—LOST LINES:—
LMR
NIGEL WELBOURN

IAN ALLAN
Publishing

C O N T E N T S

First published 1994
ISBN 0 7110 2277 1

Published by Ian Allan Publishing an imprint of Ian Allan Ltd, Terminal House, Station Approach, Shepperton, Surrey TW17 8AS; and printed by Ian Allan Printing Ltd, Coombelands House, Coombelands Lane, Addlestone, Weybridge, Surrey KT15 1HY.

ACKNOWLEDGEMENTS
I would like to thank all those who helped me with this book.
In particular, I would like to thank my parents whose patience and understanding when I was younger allowed me to visit so many lines that are now closed.
I would also like to thank all those courteous and helpful railwaymen and women who once worked on the lines mentioned in this book.

The lines of John Betjeman's *Great Central Railway Sheffield Victoria to Banbury* are reproduced from his *Collected Poems* by permission of John Murray (Publishers) Ltd.

Nigel P. Welbourn DIP TP, DIP TS, MRTPI, FRGS.

Cover photos:
Colour-Rail

Right: 'Black 5' No 44910 departs from Liverpool Exchange with the 9.50am express for Edinburgh and Glasgow on 4 June 1967. *P. Gerald*

Introduction

The London Midland Region is the third book in the series 'The Lost Lines'. A cross-section of closed lines and stations have been selected for this volume, for their regional interest, together with their historical and geographical associations.

In 1923, by amalgamation of smaller companies, the railways of Great Britain were grouped into the 'big four': the London Midland and Scottish Railway (LMS), the London and North Eastern Railway, the Great Western Railway and the Southern Railway. When these private companies were nationalised in 1948, the whole system created and called 'British Railways' was divided into six regions for convenience of control and administration. The largest of the new regions was the London Midland which was broadly the old LMS without Scotland. The other regions were the Western, Scottish, Southern, Eastern and North Eastern.

With some exceptions, this series of books is broadly based on the regional boundaries that were established in 1948. This is because at that time the boundaries selected more closely fitted the earlier constituent companies than those finally arrived at after a number of alterations.

Although there had been some closures, at their formation the six regions covered one of the most comprehensive railway networks in the world. Yet it was clear, even then, that the changing trends in economic and travel patterns were not truly reflected in the distribution of lines. The problem was compounded in that after heavy World War 2 use, the equip-

ment on many lines was life-expired. Thus it was that the railways at nationalisation had substantial arrears in both maintenance and investment.

The ever increasing competitive edge of road transport meant that the railways were no longer in a particularly sound position and British Railways fell ever deeper into debt. As a consequence in the 1960s notice was served that the complete railway network, which had survived relatively intact up to that time, would be scrutinised as never before. In particular in financial terms the contribution of individual lines would be examined and it was clear many would be unlikely to survive. In a surprisingly short time, before the brake on closures was applied, the system was irrevocably reduced in size. By the end of the 1970s over 8,000 miles of line had been closed, equivalent to the diameter of the world. The lost lines were created on a unprecedented scale.

In the knowledge that change was inevitable, in the 1960s I started to record my travels by train and in the subsequent years I eventually covered, with a few exceptions, every passenger line on each of the six regions. The railway network is much smaller than when I first set out and indeed the London Midland and other regions were abandoned after over 40 years of geographical division in favour of other means of organisation. Yet as this book shows, much survives; indeed the earthworks and structures of abandoned lines have a fascination in themselves; lost but not forgotten.

1 Historical perspective

London Midland Region could claim its roots were in the Industrial Revolution and the associated development of a number of early mineral lines. The Mansfield and Pinxton Railway, which first conveyed coal over its line in 1819 and later carried Mansfield stone to build the Houses of Parliament, and the Leicester and Swannington Railway which opened, between Leicester and Bagworth, in 1832 were two early examples. In addition to mineral wealth, the region also contained some of the great English cities whose rapid development owed much to the railway such as Birmingham, Liverpool and Manchester and it was between London and these cities that the first real main lines developed.

It was the Liverpool and Manchester Railway, opened in 1830 and engineered by George Stephenson, that can be regarded as the first modern passenger railway to link two cities by steam power. It was therefore fitting that the region's last official steam train should run between those cities in 1968. Yet it was the 112-mile London and Birmingham Railway opened throughout in 1838 which was per-

haps the finest example of an early trunk line. This route, together with the Grand Junction Railway which linked Birmingham to Liverpool and Manchester, formed a backbone of later railway development in the region. In time the numerous independent railway lines began to merge and consolidate to form a number of well-known railway companies prior to the 1923 Grouping.

There was the London and North Western Railway (LNWR), which was formed in 1846 largely from an

Below: The lost gateway to the region. The outstanding pure classical monument to railway history was the Euston Doric Arch which was completed in 1838. This view was taken in June 1957. It is now generally considered that its demolition in 1962 was one of the most wanton acts of architectural vandalism ever committed. The iron gates are preserved at York Railway Museum. *British Railways*

Right: A guard in his uniform of the London and North Western Railway. Note the buttonhole, all part of the 'Premier Line's' image. *British Railways*

amalgamation of the early main lines mentioned above. It became known as the 'Premier Line', and the solid brick structures, smart staff and respectable economic performance all added credence to its self-assumed title. It ran on the West Coast main line the whole length of what was to become the London Midland Region, from London to Carlisle. It handled the Scottish and Irish mail, and the 'blackberry' livery of its engines was perpetuated by British Railways' standard black livery up to the last day of steam.

The Midland Railway (MR), which styled itself as 'The Best Way', was the third largest of the pre-Grouping railways and was for a time noted for the excellence of its stations and carriages. This railway also eventually ran from London to Carlisle, but via

Above right: The LMS Coat of Arms. Unlike many of the pre-Grouping company crests, this was a simple device with symbols, perhaps not unexpectedly, representing London, England and Scotland. *British Railways*

Right: A welcome change in attitude towards railway heritage has now generally emerged. As part of the restoration works carried out at Manchester Victoria station, the tile map of the former Lancashire and Yorkshire Railway network was cleaned and restored to its former glory as this photograph taken in November 1979 shows. *R. G. Fox*

Above: The LMS diversified into other means of transport. This brand new AEC Reliance bus of the late 1920s was limited to 20mph. *Ian Allan Library*

Left: World War 2 left its mark, not only in heavy traffic with minimum maintenance, but also in structural damage such as this at Manchester Victoria station, which was never fully restored to its original condition. *Ian Allan Library*

the Midlands and over the Pennines from Settle to Carlisle. Apart from passengers, it carried immense amounts of coal and beer and its rich crimson livery eventually became the maroon of the London Midland and Scottish Railway (LMS).

The Great Central Railway (GCR) also ran from London to a number of the towns served by the Midland Railway and the railways were rivals right up to the days when the LMS ran the Midland main line and the LNER the Great Central. Eventually in the 1950s the Great Central's route was merged within the London Midland Region (LMR). This competitor, perhaps not too surprisingly, became an eventual candidate for closure by the LMR. In its day the Great

Central Railway was a very fine railway, but it is also true that the London extension to Marylebone had insufficient justification and never developed the income anticipated.

Then there was the Lancashire and Yorkshire Railway (LYR), the 'Lanky' with its high Victorian and in some cases slightly forbidding stations. It was an efficient railway serving the numerous Lancashire towns, uniting them with towns in Yorkshire and running to the Lancashire coast. In 1922 it amalgamated with the London and North Western Railway and therefore was not technically incorporated into the LMS in 1923.

Numerous other smaller companies also existed.

Right: On Thursday 1 January 1948 the private railways of Britain passed into national ownership. This view shows a 'Nationalisation' poster being put up in Manchester on 30 December 1947. *Topical Press*

Below right: A decline in traffic such as this was another reason for mounting deficits. The caption on this 1950s photograph reads, 'Senior porter George Jones stacks the last parcel into a van containing about 800 packages for Birmingham. Nine trains of parcels leave Oldham every night.' *British Railways*

They included the North Staffordshire Railway (NSR) serving the Potteries and nearby countryside, the Furness Railway (FR) which served the southern Lake District, and the North London Railway (NLR) which, although technically for most of its life part of the London and North Western Railway, appeared with a separate identity.

In order to strengthen the weaker companies they were grouped with the stronger ones on 1 January 1923, when the London Midland and Scottish Railway (LMS) was born. Its territory within England was formed primarily by a merger of the companies mentioned above, with the exception of the GCR. At its formation the LMS was an awe-inspiring organisation and was one of the world's largest companies. It operated in 32 of the 40 English counties and until the end of the 1930s had more staff than the British Army. At first the LMS operated in sub-regions based broadly on the areas of its original constituents. Amongst its trunk routes was the former London and North Western line to Scotland running from London as far as Carlisle. Branching off this line were routes to Manchester, Liverpool, North Wales and Birmingham. It also, as the name suggests, inherited the bulk of the Midland Railway's lines.

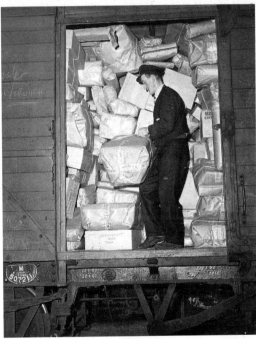

Although the LMS was unkindly referred to by some as the 'Lazy Man's Service', in fact it was for the most part an efficient and forward looking organisation. However, in the 1930s the financial situation of the LMS was already beginning to deteriorate, due largely to increasing road competition, and about thirty branch lines were closed to passengers early in that decade. Freight receipts, particularly from coal, remained considerable, but the company could already see that the finances of many of its secondary lines were not healthy. Consequently, investment on such lines was a low priority. Indeed it was hardly as an act of faith in the future of rail, that the LMS was an early investor in bus companies such as Midland Red and others. World War 2 meant that exceedingly heavy traffic with the minimum of maintenance compounded the problems and there was therefore widespread relief at Nationalisation in 1948.

Above: Bury Knowsley Street on 4 April 1971, just six months after withdrawal of services on the Bolton to Rochdale line. Demolition was soon under way, but today not all is lost as the East Lancashire Railway runs through the site. *R. J. Farrell*

The newly nationalised 'British Railways' was divided for administrative reasons into regions and thus came into operation the London Midland Region (LMR). The influence of the former LMS on this new region was considerable and in many ways, for a time, it was the old LMS without Scotland. The region at its vesting date inherited almost 5,000 route miles, making it the largest of the six new regions. The new regional colour was a rather muddy maroon.

This big and rather run-down region had an unfortunate inheritance, many of its stations having seen no significant investment for years. Typically many were soot covered, the flaking paint, murky rooms and subways still lit by gas, even in the 1960s. Coupled with some population movement out of parts of the region, increased competition from road transport and decline in the region's industrial base, there was clear evidence of overcapacity, life-expired equipment and the need for change.

From the early Fifties the car began to change the long-term balance of travel and the railways began to fall ever deeper into the red. It was inevitable that the Midland Region which had incorporated much worn out infrastructure and a number of internal competing lines, including no fewer than three main lines to Manchester, would have to question its route mileage.

In 1961 Dr Richard Beeching became Chairman of the British Railways Board with a mandate to make a substantial reduction in the losses. The report under his leadership in 1963 identified many lines in the Midland Region for closure. There were some notable reprieves, such as the former LNWR Manchester to Buxton line, but the implementation of his policy saw massive closures within the region during the 1960s. This provides the context for many of those lost lines considered in this book.

Eventually, the closures were brought to a virtual end and in the 1970s and 1980s far fewer lines were lost. What then of the future? As a planner, much of my time is spent looking at the future nature of change. In the context of railways I put forward a particularly optimistic long-term scenario. Growth in travel cannot be sustained without an appropriate contribution from a larger and better used rail network. The former London Midland Region contains a number of significant urban areas; the revival may be seen first in these areas. I wager that, to meet the travel needs of Britain, trains will eventually return to some of the closed lines included in this book.

2 Geography of the region

For the purposes of this book, with the exception of much of the ex-GCR main line which was added to the LMR in the 1950s, the region's boundaries selected are broadly those at Nationalisation as the boundaries at that time were roughly coterminous with the old railway companies that the region replaced. In other later changes a number of lines were transferred from the Western Region to the London Midland Region in areas of the West Midlands and North Wales as far south as Aberystwyth, in a quid pro quo for the Western Region annexing many of the Southern Region's lines in the South West.

From its two main stations in London, Euston and St Pancras, the LMR stretched northwards to the Scottish border at Carlisle. It ran through extremes of countryside. Travelling north from London it passed through the Thames basin and Home Counties to cover, as its name implied, the Midland plains including Birmingham and the Potteries. It fanned out to include the remote mountainous areas of North Wales and the island of Anglesey. In contrast it also served the Derbyshire, Nottinghamshire, North Staffordshire and Lancashire coalfields, together with industrial areas and major cities such as Liverpool and Manchester to the west of the Pennines. It operated over the mountainous Pennines and the beautiful and remote Lake District.

A rich variety of landscapes, stations and engineering achievements was covered by the region, which boasted several notable viaducts and the largest number of tunnels of all the regions. The region also contained a hugely diverse architectural heritage, the great mass of designs reflecting the many changes of materials and landscapes in the area that it covered. Although lack of new investment may have helped to cause some lost lines, equally it left a legacy in many areas of structures largely unchanged since they were built by the original companies.

Above: Map of Regional Boundaries 1958. *Ian Allan Library*

Next page top: The London Midland Region inherited more tunnels than any other, including about 50 that were over a half a mile in length. There were also many shorter tunnels such as this at Haslingden on the steeply inclined and now closed line from Stubbins Junction to Accrington. This photograph was taken in May 1970 after closure of the line in December 1966. *R. K. Graham*

Next page below: The region contained great variations in countryside. Dwarfed by a deep limestone cutting in the Peak District, a Stanier '8F' 2-8-0 No 48744 bursts out of a tunnel near Peak Forest Junction with a Buxton to Glazebrook freight on 19 February 1968. *G. E. Tatto Brown*

Broad Street

As London grew on its northern outskirts, suburban traffic increased and the North London Railway, although in fact for most of its life forming part of the LNWR, saw opportunities in extending southwards from Dalston to the City of London. Thus it was that the City terminus for the North London Railway at Broad Street was opened for passengers in November 1865 and for goods in May 1868.

The suburban traffic handled by the new station grew at a phenomenal rate. The line into Broad Street was quadrupled by 1874 and eventually nine platforms were provided. Traffic continued to develop until the turn of the century and at one time the number of passengers handled at Broad Street during the morning peak was surpassed only at Liverpool Street.

Broad Street was particularly distinctive. The terminus was built in a mixture of Italian, slightly oriental and 'town hall' styles, complete with clock tower, to designs by William Baker, engineer of the North London Railway. However, by the time the passenger terminus closed, the design had been seriously disfigured. The frontage had been considerably altered by

the LNWR who in 1913 built a very plain entrance façade between the road and the main station. This was constructed of Portland stone, completely out of context with the texture and design of the original building.

The World War 2 blitz of London caused considerable damage to the station. This was never properly repaired and added to the increasingly shabby appearance of the station. Later the LMR built obtrusive and out of character platform entrances and facilities on the concourse. Finally, in the 1960s the mansard style train sheds were crudely cut back. Nevertheless, the Italian styled staircase with attractive marble columns on the eastern side of the station

Below: Broad Street in busier days. This view taken in the late 1950s shows Broad Street as it was seldom seen in later years. Note the sign indicating platform No 9. This was outside the main train shed, having been the last platform added in 1919. *British Railways*

Above: Outside the peak hours there was little activity. Even in the mid-1960s, when this view of electric multiple units (EMUs) was taken, there were more coaches than passengers. Note the bars at the windows due to limited clearances on the line. *British Railways*

Left: An almost deserted Broad Street concourse looking east towards Liverpool Street in July 1975. Note the war memorial which was a miniature version of the Cenotaph in Whitehall. *K. Lane*

survived to the end. The staircase connection from nearby Liverpool Street led up to the first floor concourse of Broad Street.

Few passengers were ever spotted on the concourse during the last days of the station and those that were found were sometimes lost, thinking Broad Street was a part of Liverpool Street. The buffet and shops had shut several years before the station itself closed. A crude sign had been daubed on the wall indicating that phones could be found. It seems unlikely that any more official damage or neglect could have been done to this potentially splendid building. Only three of the platforms were used in the end, which together with the state of the disused goods yard created a large area of dereliction in the City of London.

Underneath the station there was a vast catacomb of tunnels and arches which were used in their last days for car parking. This area was strangely sinister. Perhaps it was haunted by the ghosts of those who had been murdered on this line in Victorian times, whose deaths had resulted in the communication cord being developed.

Broad Street had seen decades of decline as the tram and later the bus took their toll. The decline was arrested for a while when the line was electrified in 1921, but the downward drift soon continued. Watford services became peak period only in 1962, whilst in 1963 the station was one of the few in London

Top: An attractive, if not entirely convenient, hike up to the station was by this staircase which led from street level to the Broad Street concourse. This view was taken in the summer of 1977 and shows the cluttered station entrance looked down upon by a fine Venetian styled window. *Author*

Above: The area beneath the station was for a time used for car parking, together with the former goods yard. This view in 1977 shows the extent and interesting architecture of the catacombs below the station. *Author*

Above right: At the top of the stairs linking the station to street level and Liverpool Street was a notice suggesting that it was unlikely that your destination would be served from Broad Street station. *A. G. Merrells.*

Above left: A view of Broad Street station on 18 February 1978. The overall roof has been cut back to the extent that it provides little protection for passengers in wet weather. A three-car EMU waits to leave for Richmond. *J. Vaughan*

Left: A train arrives at Broad Street station on 26 January 1982. By this time only four platforms were in use. A view that was to see considerable change. *M. Bond*

Above: Broad Street No 2 signalbox on 4 April 1986 with demolition in progress all round. The box was the last to remain at the station, even after the nearby track had been lifted. Perhaps it was the lucky horseshoe near the front entrance. *A. Dasi-Sutton*

Right: Close-up of one of the main parts of the terminal building crudely attacked by demolition contractors. The hoarding cannot hide the extent of the devastation when this view was taken on 11 July 1985. *R. Norman*

proposed for closure in the Beeching Report. It was reprieved in 1965, but closed to goods in January 1969. A survey in 1971 indicated that daily passenger departures had reduced to 4,800 which was unfairly compared to over 93,000 at Liverpool Street. Closure was finally agreed in June 1985 and demolition began soon after.

A single temporary platform was provided on the site until June the following year when the last link to Dalston Junction was closed and remaining trains were for a time diverted into Liverpool Street. Broad Street station has completely disappeared, the site having been comprehensively redeveloped, but retaining a vestige in the name Broadgate.

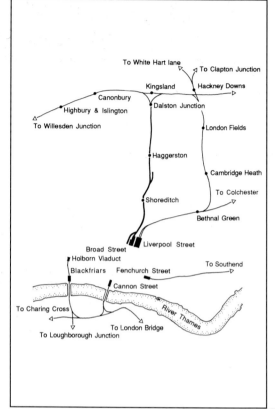

Below: Soon after demolition began the site of Broad Street station was completely cleared and today the site is unrecognisable, in use as a major City office development. Although Liverpool Street survived, the clock tower in this view, which before World War 2 had a spire, did not survive the redevelopment. *A. C. Mott*

4 Last years of the Great Central main line

The Great Central's extension to London from Annesley in Nottinghamshire was completed in March 1899. It was the last main line to reach London, but today it is a lost main line to the north.

The extension resulted in a line that ran as a spine through England from London north via Aylesbury and on through Quainton Road, Brackley, Rugby, Leicester and Loughborough to Nottingham. The line

Right: The last day of the Great Central main line. Enthusiasts crowd round one of the last steam trains to leave Marylebone on 3 September 1966, pulled by a Stanier 'Black 5' 4-6-0 No 45292 heading the 4.38pm train to Nottingham Victoria.
K. Lawrence

Below: Calvert station, north of Aylesbury, with track laying in progress in July 1966.
A. Muckley

Left: 'Black 5' No 44872 enters gas-lit Brackley Central in Northamptonshire on a Nottingham to Neasden parcels train. The vans had travelled up the night before laden with newspapers. The date is 2 September 1966, just one day before closure. *J. M. French*

Below: The demolished station at Helmdon looking north towards Woodford Halse in March 1966. Note the overgrown trackside flowerbeds. *A. Muckley*

then joined with that to Sheffield and went over the Pennines in the original dual Woodhead Tunnels which were in excess of 3 miles in length, to arrive at Manchester, over 200 miles from Marylebone.

The engineering of the London extension was of outstanding quality with minimum grades and curvature to allow high speed running. The line was also built to the wider continental loading gauge, capable of taking the largest locomotives as it was originally intended that this railway should form part of a

Right: Brackley Central, or 'Top station' as it was sometimes known locally, is now used as a garage. This view was taken on 30 January 1994. *Author*

Below: Woodford station in Great Central days. The platform on the left was for the spur to Stratford-upon-Avon. *Locomotive Publishing Co*

through route to the continent via a proposed Channel Tunnel, a realisation that only recently became feasible.

It was a modern railway, both fast and punctual, and the first to adopt automatic colour light signalling. None the less, although provision was made for growth at stations such as Nottingham Victoria and Marylebone, traffic never grew to anything approaching their capacity or expectations and the new Marylebone terminus was one of London's

quieter stations. Indeed it was in stark contrast to St Pancras, the Midland Railway's rival, both in usage and in that it was built austerely compared with the huge Gothic opulence of St Pancras.

Also in contrast to Marylebone station was the adjacent hotel. An attractive porte-cochère led from the very modest station to the huge Hotel Great Central which on opening in 1899 contained some 700 bedrooms. The hotel was built as an immense block with a Flemish theme to designs by Colonel Robert Edis. Most of the exterior is in a fawn terracotta and the clock tower to the Marylebone Road frontage is a well-known London landmark. The hotel was turned into offices in 1945 and for many years acted as the headquarters of the British Railways Board.

In 1923 the GCR became part of the London and North Eastern Railway and Gresley's 'A3' Pacifics were used on the top trains to compete with the LMS. However, under BR the eventual transfer of the main line, with the exception of an area around Sheffield which remained in the Eastern Region, was to the London Midland Region. The need for economy focused attention on this former London and North Eastern Railway adversary within the LMR fold. In the end any pretence at competing services to Leicester, Nottingham, Sheffield and Manchester, and to other stations served by alternative lines, was dropped. A long, calculated and acrimonious period of run down and closure was entered into. Express trains were re-routed in 1960 and an infrequent local

service of semi-fast trains was provided to serve the stations on the ex-GCR route. The few cross-country trains were gradually diverted to other routes, many local stations closed in March 1963 and the stage was set for the creation of one of the longest lost main lines.

Most freight ended in 1965 and the line closed for through passengers between Aylesbury and Sheffield in September 1966. A section between Nottingham Victoria and Rugby Central survived until May 1969, although in September 1967 trains had been cut back to Nottingham Arkwright Street. The vast

Above: A Nottingham to Marylebone DMU has emerged from the 1 mile 1,240yd long Catesby Tunnel which was completed in 1897 and has a span of 26ft. One of the tunnel's five air shafts can be seen on the horizon. *F. A. Haynes*

Left: Catesby Tunnel in the far distance is obliterated by vegetation on 30 January 1994. The hikers indicate that this stretch of former line still has its uses, silently awaiting the return of trains. *Author*

Right: BR Standard Class 9F 2-10-0 No 92030 passes over the West Coast main line with an 'up' freight at Rugby on 17 October 1964. *P. Wells*

Nottingham Victoria became a shopping complex, but mercifully this station's attractive stone and red brick clock tower was retained in the redevelopment. Demolition took place elsewhere and at one time plans were even put forward to close Marylebone station itself and to divert trains into Baker Street.

But the Great Central has its friends. Such an excellent railway with its island platforms, absence of level crossings and wide loading gauge has been consistently looked at for reopening. The Great Central Railway (1976) run a section of the line from Loughborough to a new terminus at Leicester North. At Loughborough they have constructed extensive covered accommodation and have a fine array of locomotives. There are also long-term plans to link northward to the Nottingham Heritage Centre at Ruddington.

Even the former GCR hotel at Marylebone has been reopened and refurbished as one of the most luxurious in London. Plans to close Marylebone were scrapped; instead the station was refurbished and modified. The line also lives on in John Betjeman's poem, an extract from Great Central Railway describes part of the route, between Nottingham and Rugby, as follows:

'Through cuttings deep to Nottingham
Precariously we wound;
The swallowing tunnel made the train
Seem London's Underground.
Above the fields of Leicestershire
On arches we were borne
And the rumble of the railway drowned
The thunder of the Quorn;
And silver shone the steeples out
Above the barren boughs;
Colts in a paddock ran from us
But not the solid cows;
And quite where Rugby Central is
Does only Rugby know.
We watched the empty platform wait
And sadly saw it go.'

Sadly, much of the line did go and Rugby Central's empty platform is today used as a footpath, as part of the Great Central Way. None the less, in addition to the sections preserved and those in use near Sheffield and Manchester, the line also remains open to passengers from Marylebone to Aylesbury. From here a single freight line runs northward through Quainton

Road to Calvert. Although much has been demolished, much remains. The lost line is being considered increasingly as a wasted asset and the Central Railway project has plans to reopen further sections of the line south of Leicester and to provide links on to the Channel Tunnel, fulfilling at last the London extension's original vision!

Top: Rugby Central, looking towards Nottingham in March 1966. *A. Muckley*

Above left: Rugby Central in January 1994, almost a quarter of a century after closure. *Author*

Above right: Lutterworth station, looking north in March 1966. *A. Muckley*

Above left: 'Black 5' No 45288 leaves Ashby Magna with the 6.15pm Nottingham to Rugby train on 9 May 1966. The M1 motorway is in the background. *M. Mitchell*

Left: Rothley station on the preserved section of the Great Central between Leicester North and Loughborough Central. This view taken on 18 March 1990 shows that much work has been done to restore the station to an authentic appearance including gas lighting and advertisement hoardings. *J. East*

Above: Whilst perhaps not quite historically accurate in this location and with BR coaches, preserved former LMS 'Jubilee' 4-6-0 No 5593 *Kolhapur* creates a majestic sight as it stands in Loughborough station at night on 10 November 1990. This station is on the now preserved section of line between Loughborough and Leicester North. *J. B. Gosling*

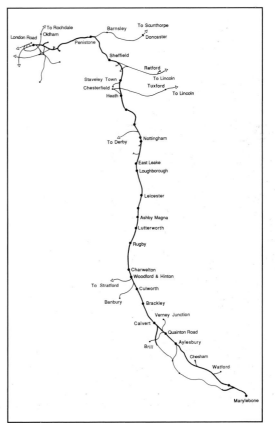

Above left: Standard Class 9F No 92042 passes beneath the cathedral-like roof of Nottingham Victoria station with a down iron ore train on 29 August 1964. *J. S. Hancock*

Left: 'Black 5' No 44858 brings stock past Victoria North signalbox for the 5.15pm train to Marylebone on 1 September 1966. *R. E. B. Siviter*

Above: The last passenger trains to use Victoria were the Nottingham to Rugby local services. Here a DMU leaves platform No 6, in the end the only one in use, with the 12.25pm to Rugby on 15 July 1967. The destination board showed Leicester as there were no Rugby blinds! *J. Cupit*

Centre right: Destination boards at Nottingham Victoria on 13 August 1966. A poster in the background reminds passengers that the Midland station is the one for fast services to London. *E. Wilmshurst*

Below right: Former Great Central signal and view looking south at Nottingham Victoria on 12 March 1966, little had changed in this scene since the station opened. *E. Wilmshurst*

⑤ Buckingham and beyond

The Buckinghamshire Railway opened the 30½ mile line from Bletchley to Banbury, via Buckingham and Brackley, throughout in May 1850. It ran through the gentle hills and some of the less populated agricultural areas of Buckinghamshire, Northamptonshire and Oxfordshire. The terminus at Banbury Merton Street was located near the town's important cattle market and GWR station. It was an economically constructed small-scale terminus, built largely of wood, with an elliptical overall roof which covered part of its two platforms. The roof in its final years was stripped of its cladding for most of its length.

At Verney Junction, where a station was opened in September 1868, the line from Bletchley to Banbury divided. As the junction of the line was unrelated to any settlement it took its name from a local landowner and MP associated with the railway, Sir Harry Verney. A small settlement and public house grew up, known even today as Verney Junction. The second 21¾ mile line from the junction opened in May 1851 and ran via Bicester to Oxford Rewley Road station. This Oxford terminus, which still partly remains as a garage, is unique in being built to the same prefabricated principles and by the same contractor as the Crystal Palace.

The lines were worked by the LNWR from the start as the company was anxious to prevent any possible rival incursions both to Birmingham and to Oxford. Indeed the Metropolitan Railway, which ran trains to Verney Junction, had designs on Oxford, although a line only ever ran as far west as Brill. The small town's plans of becoming a spa on a line to

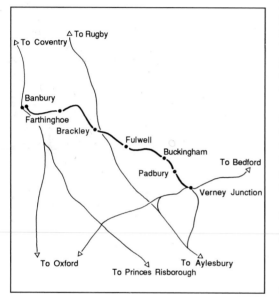

Below: The exterior of Banbury Merton Street on 13 July 1957. *M. Farr*

Above: Banbury Merton Street just before demolition on 7 September 1966. *A. Muckley*

Right: The site of Banbury Merton Street on 30 January 1994. *Author*

Oxford were unfulfilled and the Brill line closed in 1935.

Banbury was served by the GWR main line and Brackley, with its school founded in the 16th century, was served by the GCR main line. Buckingham, which lost out as the county town to Aylesbury, did not grow extensively after the railway reached the town, and the line from Verney Junction to Banbury remained a relative backwater. Decline gradually set in after World War 2 and a link from near Banbury via Towcester to Blisworth was closed in July 1951, whilst a freight line from Towcester that linked

Left: The 'Banburian', a former LNWR 0-8-0 pulls away up the grade out of Farthinghoe on the last stage of the journey to Banbury on 22 September 1962. *A. R. Butcher*

Right: Two single railcars Nos M79900/1 form the 4.30pm Banbury to Buckingham train approaching Brackley on 6 August 1960. *M. Mensing*

Left: Railcar No M79901 at Radclive, just to the west of Buckingham, one of the halts built specially for the railcar service, on 23 July 1959. *M. Farr*

through to the Buckinghamshire town of Olney closed in June 1958.

Nevertheless in 1956 the Banbury line was chosen for an experiment with single unit diesel railcars. This and the opening of two halts on the line increased patronage and revenue, but unfortunately not quite sufficiently to save the branch. The northern 16¾-mile extension from Buckingham to Banbury Merton Street closed to passengers in January 1961 and to freight in December 1963, whilst Buckingham to Verney Junction closed to passengers the following September and to freight in December 1966. The track was lifted the following year and the station buildings have subsequently been demolished.

The line through Verney Junction remained open between Oxford and Bletchley for freight until 1993

Left: A view of the loading gauge and bay taken in 1982. *Author*

Below: In January 1994 the loading gauge remained, but had been completely covered with ivy; it can just be made out in this view. The growth of vegetation has been such that a Tree Preservation Order has been confirmed on the site. *Author*

Right: A westbound freight approaching Verney Junction on 27 February 1960 hauled by Stanier 8F No 48551. In 1994 only two platform faces and a single mothballed rusting line remain at this location. *S. Rickard*

Below right: Verney Junction, looking towards Oxford in July 1966. The dovecote and gardens have long since gone. *A. Muckley*

when the section east of Bicester Town station was mothballed. However, the Bicester to Claydon section was reopened for freight in January 1994 to utilise once again the connection to the Calvert disposal point on the former GCR main line.

Above: Verney Junction signalbox and, branching off to the right, the Buckingham line which by the time this view was taken in July 1966 was freight-only. Today the signalbox and Buckingham line have gone and a single rusting mothballed line runs through the site. *A. Muckley*

Left: Oxford Rewley Road, one of the few stations on the line to survive. This view of part of the train shed was taken in September 1989. *Author*

Above right: Ex-LMS Class 2 4-4-0 No 40646 and a Fowler 2-6-2T pass through Olney station on a rail tour from Birmingham on 14 April 1962, shortly after the station had closed to regular passenger traffic. *D. E. Esau*

Right: A view taken in the early 1980s after demolition of the station and clearance of the site. *Author*

⑥ Bedfordshire byways

Bedford St John's

Bedford has been associated with transport from early times, developing at a ford on the River Ouse. The river was for many years the established means of transporting freight eastward to King's Lynn and Yarmouth. Thus it was that when the first railway to the town opened in November 1846 it ran to the west, connecting with the main line at Bletchley and soon becoming part of the LNWR. In May 1857 the Midland reached the town by extending their line

Left: St John's station before major demolition had taken place, but after electric lights had been installed. *L. Turner*

Below: Bedford St John's station in LMS days. Note the Southern poster board. *V. R. Anderson*

Above: A similar view, but with a DMU on a Cambridge to Oxford train pausing at the station, which still has gas-lit platforms in July 1966. *A. Muckley*

Below: St John's on 21 July 1979 with a DMU in the station. The line in the foreground led to Bedford Midland via the main line; note the old signal. When Bedford St John's closed on 12 May 1984 a new halt was opened 250yd to the north and the spur line in the foreground was lifted. *S. Creer*

Above: A DMU waits with the 16.15 train to Bletchley at Bedford St John's on 6 May 1981. The station buildings have been reduced to an absolute minimum.
Brian Morrison

Left: The remains of Bedford St John's on 16 February 1988. The distant signalbox still remains and the area has yet to be redeveloped in 1994. *K. Lane*

Right: A DMU on the 11.45am Hitchin to Bedford train about to enter Old Warden Tunnel on 7 June 1960. *P. Thatcher*

Below: Leighton Buzzard narrow gauge sand lines at the Double Arches sand quarry, still in use in April 1978. *D. Cox*

south to Hitchin through Bedford from Leicester.

The Midland wanted their new station at Bedford to be sited jointly with the LNWR at St John's, but the local council preferred a new site to the north of this existing station. The line to Bletchley was subsequently extended to both Oxford and Cambridge; St John's station primarily served this cross-country route. However, ensuing closures resulted in only the original Bedford to Bletchley section remaining open for passengers and the use of St John's was much reduced. Finally, by the use of some tight mainly freight curves, remaining trains were diverted into the former Midland station and St John's closed in May 1984, although its name is perpetuated in a nearby halt.

A link to the Cross

The opening of the present Midland main line to London St Pancras in 1868 meant that the original 16¾-mile line from Bedford to Hitchin, which relied on using GNR tracks into London King's Cross, soon fell into decline. The line crossed the LNWR branch from Bletchley to Bedford near St John's station and in March 1875 ill fate struck a blow when Midland and LNWR trains collided at this point. The line also contained some steep gradients, particularly out of Bedford up to Old Warden Tunnel, which was 880yd long. The route had been singled, except for a section between Southill and Shefford, as far back as World War 1. DMUs were later introduced, but in spite of this the line closed to passengers at the end of December 1961. The track near Cardington, which served the nearby RAF base, was used for a little longer, but the line was finally lifted in 1964. The route contains some fine and very typical Midland architecture at one of its intermediate stations, Southill, which is still in use as a private residence, whilst the tunnel at Old Warden is one of the very few disused in South East England.

The Silver Sands

The famous Leighton Buzzard Silver Sand is one of up to thirty different varieties and grades of sand that could be found in a single pit in the area and the unique Silver Sand has been exported to many areas, including Arabia! It was the growth of this sand industry which resulted in the development of a unique network of 2ft narrow gauge lines which ran from Leighton Buzzard to serve mineral sites to the northeast of the town.

Above: Derelict wagons to the north of Stonehenge Works in the early 1980s. *Author*

Right: Much of the Leighton Buzzard narrow gauge system is now in use as a preserved railway for passenger traffic. 0-4-0WT (Well Tank) *P. C. Allen* rounds a curve on the line near Marley's Bank in a sylvan setting in July 1971. *P. H. Groom*

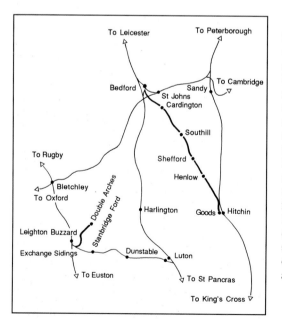

The Leighton Buzzard Railway system was opened in November 1919 to connect sand pits in the area to central washeries and to the exchange sidings on the standard gauge Leighton Buzzard to Dunstable branch line. At their peak the narrow gauge lines carried over 500 wagons of sand a day to the exchange sidings, but never formed part of the LMR. After the early 1950s this rail traffic dwindled and in 1969 the exchange sidings at Leighton Buzzard were closed, together with the remaining section of the branch to Dunstable. The last commercial delivery using the narrow gauge system was made in 1977, but internal sand trains remained on short sections for some time further. Today passenger trains are operated by the Leighton Buzzard Railway and run on almost 3 miles of line from Page's Park to Stonehenge Works. A splendid range of engines has been collected, not only from this country, but also from much further afield.

7 Rutland in retrospect

Rutland was once England's smallest county and perhaps one of the least spoilt. It was a minor version of the Cotswolds with its geology reflected in its buildings and at one time providing a number of ironstone lines. One such example is the Cottesmore Iron Ore Mines Siding which is now home to the Rutland Railway Museum and dedicated mainly to portraying the iron ore industry. It was not a heavily populated area and although crossed by three pre-Grouping railway companies, growth at junctions such as Seaton, Manton and Luffenham was decidedly restrained. The county is no more, together with a number of lines that once ran within its area.

Much of the county was within the LMR and the

Left: Ex-LMS 'Tilbury Tank' 4-4-2T No 41975 waits with an Uppingham branch train at Seaton on 23 April 1959. *H. C. Casserley*

Below: BR Standard Class 2 2-6-2T No 84005 leaves Seaton with the 5.57pm to Stamford on 18 May 1964. This is not double track, but two single lines with that on the right of the view being the Uppingham branch. *G. D. King*

Left: Ivatt Class 2 2-6-2T No 41278 (incidentally of shed 2A Rugby, Seaton sub-shed) seen here leaving Seaton with the 2.45pm Uppingham train on 15 September 1956. In the background can be seen Harringworth Viaduct carrying the ex-Midland London to Nottingham line which is still in use over the viaduct for freight traffic. *P. Wells*

Below: Ivatt Class 2 No 41320 on a two-coach train at the Uppingham terminus. *David Lawrence*

former Midland main line from Nottingham crossed it dividing at Manton for London and Peterborough. Manton acted very successfully as the Midland's station for Uppingham, whose well known public school dates from the 16th century. Yet it was the ex-LNWR link from Seaton to Uppingham which eventually provided a more central station in Uppingham. Seaton was a junction which already provided services to Stamford via Luffenham, to Market Harborough and to Peterborough when the Uppingham branch was connected to the junction, opening in October 1894. It was one of the last passenger lines constructed in the area and provided a central station in Uppingham. The short 3½-mile single line to the town branched off to the north-east of Seaton and was forced to curve sharply westward, almost back on itself, in its climb out of the Welland Valley. The branch line prudently utilised two existing bridges on the Midland route

Right: Ex-LMS Class 4F 0-6-0 No 44414 heading the RCTS railtour away from Uppingham on 18 May 1963. *G. D. King*

Below: Standard Class 2 tank No 84008 at Morcott halt with the 12.40pm from Seaton to Stamford. *P. Wells*

and, once opened, Seaton and Uppingham station was renamed just as Seaton.

The Uppingham passenger service, with its somewhat inconvenient change of train, was withdrawn in June 1960. Specials to Uppingham School and freight lasted until May 1964. The Seaton to Luffenham link ended in June 1966, together with the former LNWR line from Market Harborough to Peterborough via Seaton. Today part of the eastern end of this line at Peterborough is operated by the Nene Valley Railway. Seaton station is now in private occupation, whilst Uppingham station is the site of an industrial estate.

Manton station was closed for passengers in June 1966, although the former Midland line is still used by Leicester to Peterborough trains, whilst the former main line south of Manton remains open for freight. This section of line contains the Harringworth Viaduct over the broad valley of the River Welland.

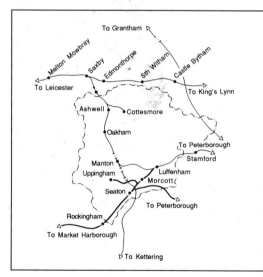

Above: Standard Class 2 tank No 84005 with the Stamford branch train at Seaton on 20 March 1965. *M. Mitchell*

Left: Three-car DMU with the 2pm for Birmingham New Street at Seaton on 13 February 1965. No 84008 waits with the Stamford branch auto train on the left. *P. Wells*

Opened in 1880 it is a staggering 1,275yd long with 82 arches, the longest in rural Britain. A clear view of the viaduct was obtained from Seaton station. Awaiting a connection on a warm summer's day at this remote station, with always the chance of seeing some interesting freight train and with a steam engine simmering in the background, was one of the delights of rail travel that is long since lost.

Right: Brush Type 2 D5638 entering Seaton with the 2.40pm Peterborough East train on 5 December 1964. *P. Wells*

Below: Seaton station almost two decades after closure, in private occupation seen here on 26 February 1985. *W. A. Sharman*

Left: A Fairburn Tank, Class 4 2-6-4T No 42087 and 'Black 5' No 45238 standing at Manton with an RCTS rail tour on 18 May 1963. *G. D. King*

Below: Seaton 1905. *Crown Copyright*

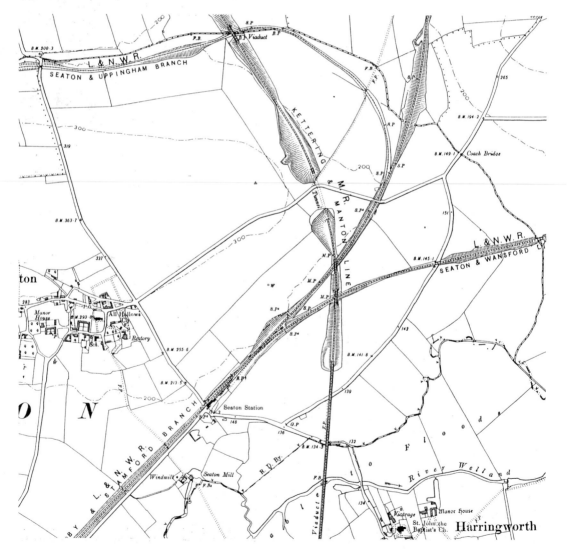

⑧ The ghost of Glenfield

The line from Desford Junction to Leicester West Bridge was opened as part of the Leicester and Swannington Railway in July 1832. Its primary purpose was to bring coal more economically from collieries to the west of Leicester into the city. This early line ran through the 1 mile 36yd long Glenfield Tunnel on its 16-mile route from West Bridge at Leicester to Swannington. The route and the tunnel were engineered by George and Robert Stephenson. The tunnel was the earliest of any consequence built specifically for a railway. It was completely straight and almost dead level, but was of a fairly narrow single bore, without any wall refuges. This caused difficulties in operation from the very first day, in that engines had to be modified to travel through it.

Indeed the first engine to run through the tunnel, called *Comet,* had its chimney almost knocked off and many of the passengers sitting in open trucks on the first ceremonial run were covered in soot. George Stephenson, driving the engine himself, brought the train to a halt near some water where passengers could clean themselves up prior to lunch. It was also reported that later, as a result of an accident with a horse and cart at a level crossing, a local musical instrument maker was commissioned to equip the engines on the line with 'steam horns'. As a result the first steam whistles were born.

The Midland Railway took over the line in 1846, which was subsequently extended to Burton upon Trent, but as traffic increased so the single bore

Glenfield Tunnel also became an increasing operating difficulty. The problem was eventually solved by avoiding the tunnel and by constructing a new loop line into Leicester, although retaining the West Bridge yard and the original line through the tunnel for freight.

Above: A short section of an old mineral incline last used in 1947 has been relaid at Spring Lane near Swannington as a reminder of the area's industrial heritage. This view was taken on 6 September 1993. *Author*

Left: Ex-MR Class 3 0-6-0 No 43728 running round the 'Charnwood Forester' special train at Swannington on 14 April 1957. *N. C. Simmons*

When the BR Standard Class 2 engines replaced the former Midland locomotives on the line it was necessary to trim the corners of the cabs, but even so clearance in the tunnel was very tight. Even when diesels were introduced on the line a pair of Standard Class 2s were retained because of the width limitations. It was said locally that it was the ghost of Stephenson which kept the steam engines running when everything else in the area was diesel.

Although the line was the oldest part of the Midland Railway and the section through the tunnel closed for passengers as far back as September 1928, the section from Desford to Leicester West Bridge

Bottom left: Ex-MR No 58209 on a special train at the western entrance to Glenfield Tunnel on the 14 April 1957. The 1 mile 26yd long bore had a span of only 11ft 6in which prevented the BR mark 1 coaches from proceeding through the tunnel. Brake van tours were provided before the line closed.
N. C. Simmons

Right: A similar view of the western end of Glenfield Tunnel on 6 September 1993. *Author*

Below: The end of the line, West Bridge Yard, Leicester from a Standard Class 2 2-6-0 No 78028 on Friday, 16 July 1965. *H. A. Gamble*

lasted until April 1966 for freight. Today Glenfield station and the western entrance to the tunnel form the site of a housing development appropriately called Stephenson Close. A plaque provides a cross-section of the old station platform and buildings, and the tunnel portal remains, although sealed by doors. Leicester West Bridge station has also been partly reconstructed and is now a public park. At Swannington, the other end of the original line, the station buildings have also been demolished, but part of the route of an old connecting mineral incline, last used in 1947, has been restored where it crosses Spring Lane. There are proposals to reopen the Leicester to Burton freight line for passengers, but of course avoiding the old tunnel section, so any ghost of Glenfield will not be disturbed.

⑨ The Midland to Mansfield

Nottingham expanded rapidly in Victorian times and indeed the first large organised rail excursion was made from the town to Leicester in July 1840. The original trades of lace and hosiery were helped by Nottingham's location on the River Trent which provided transport to the coast. The arrival of the railway allowed greater flexibility and diversification, whilst the associated coalfield also grew significantly with the coming of the railways.

Lines radiated from Nottingham over the entire coalfield. The distinctive Midland style stations and signalboxes put an indelible mark on the county. One interesting line was the Midland's Nottingham to Mansfield line which was built to tap the Leen Valley collieries. Mansfield had been served by a mineral railway opened as early as 1819, but the first section of the direct line from Nottingham opened with the 13¼ miles to Kirkby-in-Ashfield in October 1848. Newstead was one of the intermediate stations on this

Above left: A Fairburn Tank No 42161 at Nottingham Midland with a local train from Mansfield in September 1964. The bridge over the first carriage carried the former Great Central Railway over the Midland station at Nottingham, but has since been removed. *Author*

Above: A Fairburn Tank No 42232 at Newstead station on 11 September 1964 with a local train about to depart for Mansfield. *Author*

Left: The same view of Newstead on 8 May 1985. Today trains and a station have returned to this site, but the telegraph pole has gone! *Author*

Right: The abandoned Midland Railway signalbox at Annesley north of Newstead on 8 May 1985. All trace of the MR station has gone. *Author*

Below: An Ivatt Class 2 2-6-0 No 46501 with a Mansfield to Nottingham special, connecting with a Nottingham to London excursion, starting away from Mansfield station in February 1956. *F. Ashley*

section, the nearby Newstead Abbey being the magnificent home of Lord Byron the poet. The tranquil grounds of the abbey were in stark contrast to the rows of miners' cottages which were graphically described by D. H. Lawrence in his short stories and books set in Nottinghamshire.

The line pressed on a further 3¾ miles to reach Mansfield itself in October 1849, but it was not until June 1875 that a 22¾ mile northward extension, via Mansfield Woodhouse, to Worksop was completed. The Midland had a monopoly in the area for a while until the Great Northern Railway (GNR) and GCR built their own lines in the Leen Valley. For many years the former Midland line was a hive of activity,

the problem even in the 1950s being how to fit all the coal trains around the passenger services. Passenger decline set in after World War 2, but was due in part to a poor service. Stopping trains took about 50 minutes for the 17¼mile Nottingham to Mansfield journey. They were slow, and on occasions none too clean and subject to delays. All passenger services were withdrawn in October 1964, which cleared the line for coal freight.

Passenger closure came just as the coalfield and mines along the line was about to decline. Babbington, Annesley, Sherwood and Warsop

Above: A Fairburn Tank No 42232 passing Mansfield carriage sidings with the 12.25pm, Saturdays only, Nottingham Midland to Mansfield stopping train on 10 October 1964, the last day of these services.
J. S. Hancock

Right: The entrance to Mansfield station on 7 September 1993. Part of the remaining station building is currently used as a wine bar. Built in Mansfield stone, the shadings are undeniably similar to those of the Houses of Parliament which is also built largely with the same stone.
M. Wade

Left: An abandoned typically Midland styled railway house at Mansfield Woodhouse on 7 September 1993. *Author*

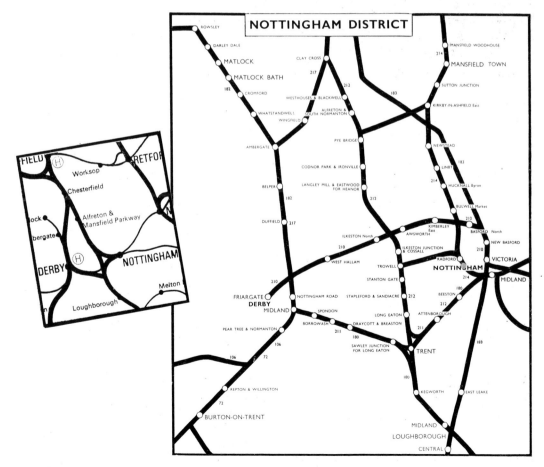

53

collieries, all with links to the line, have closed since 1981. Newstead colliery closed in 1987 and others are threatened with closure. The line north of Newstead to Kirkby-in-Ashfield was abandoned altogether, but the link from the Midland main line to Kirkby-in-Ashfield, through Mansfield and across the town on a fine viaduct to Mansfield Woodhouse and then on to Worksop, was retained for freight.

Mansfield has a population of about 60,000 and as such was the largest town in the country not to be served by a railway. My diary reported:

WEDNESDAY APRIL 28 1965; At Worksop the closed Mansfield line was still marked on the departure boards.

It was as if it could not be believed that such a large town was not still served by passenger services. In fact a Parkway station was opened on the Midland main line to resurrect the name, but it was not as successful as anticipated. Good sense prevailed and plans were made to restore passenger services to the town. The new route is known as the 'Robin Hood' line, a well-chosen title as the people of Nottinghamshire were originally robbed of this route. The line was firstly reinstated as far as Newstead and is well used. The next stage puts Mansfield back on the railway passenger map and then upgrades the existing freight route to Worksop for passenger use. Part of the stone-built station at Mansfield remains, although the overall roof and many of the original buildings have gone.

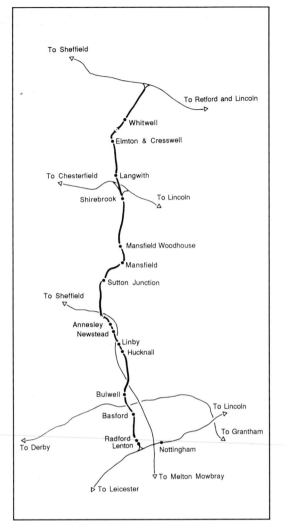

10 Gone for a Burton

Lost lines are not confined to branch and main lines. There was, particularly in industrial areas, a sizeable mileage of industrial and commercial sidings and many short connecting lines. Such lines were often privately owned and, if they survived at all, did not always come under the formal control of the main railway network.

A comprehensive number of such lines once served the various breweries in the Burton upon Trent area. Brewing was commenced in the area by the monks of Burton Abbey after they found that the local water, sharpened by gypsum, made clear and sparkling beer. William Bass opened his brewery in Burton in 1777 and others soon followed. With the arrival of the railways the town developed extensive rail freight traffic in barley and coal to the maltings, in the movement of barrels to and from the breweries and in exporting the finished ales.

To meet the increasing demand for ales, breweries extended throughout the Burton upon Trent area, but lack of space meant they could not always expand or be located close to one another. Consequently in addition to a network of lines linking to the main line railway, the various brewing processes were also often interconnected by private lines. There was much of this type of development throughout the town, the first branch opened in the early 1860s and by the 1880s a complex network of lines connected with about twenty breweries. Some idea of the scale of the railway system that developed can be gained from the

Left: Bass No 2, 0-4-0ST (Saddle Tank) with an inspection saloon on 12 April 1958 on the Burton upon Trent brewery system. *Hugh Davies*

Right: Locomotive sheds and a cross bar signal at Burton upon Trent on 12 April 1958. *Hugh Davies*

Right: 0-4-0ST Peckett being pushed back into a shed by a tractor at Burton upon Trent on 12 April 1958. *Hugh Davies*

Below centre: Preserved Bass 0-4-0ST No 9 dating from 1901 at the Bass Museum located at Burton upon Trent on 6 September 1993 *R. Trill*

Bottom: Distinctive enamel 'Beware of the Trains' signs were provided on the system. A number have been preserved such as this at the Bass Museum. *R. Trill*

Below: An example of a handlebar style of signal that operated on parts of the system and seen here preserved at the Bass Museum at Burton upon Trent on 6 September 1993. *R. Trill*

Right: Map of Burton 1924. *Crown Copyright*

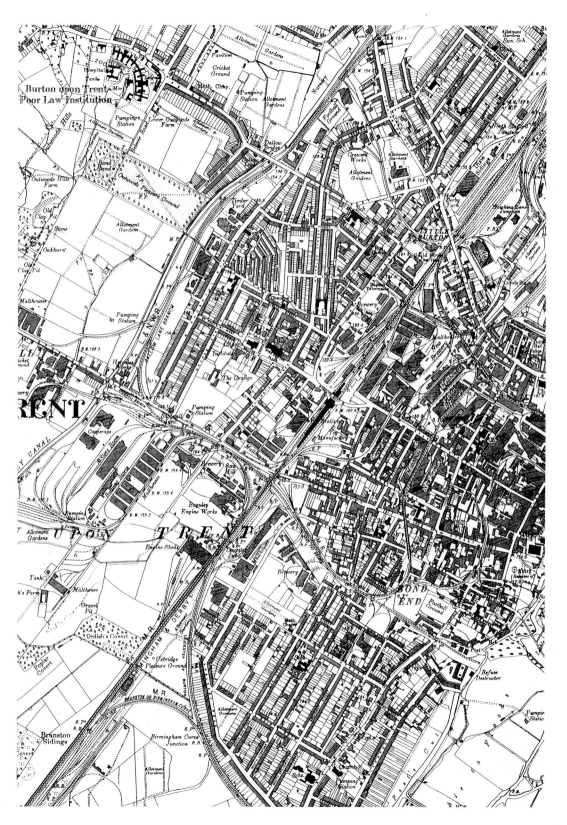

Right: The Midland Railway's grain warehouse No 2 at Burton was built in 1854. The area around the building originally embraced a coal yard, Truman's malt-houses and a turntable used by the North Staffordshire Railway. The building seen here on 6 September 1993 has recently been restored and converted to office and industrial use. *Author*

fact that Bass in the 1920s operated with their own engines over a private railway consisting of about 16 miles of line with running powers over a further 10 miles or so. At this time the system could handle about 1,000 wagons each day. Such was the extent of the system that it had its own 'main lines' signalling systems, control, timetables and an extensive number of saddle tank locomotives with distinctive combined brass domes and safety valves. The short wheelbase 0-4-0s and large buffers were designed to cope with the sharp curves on some sections of line.

There were no scheduled passenger services although special guest workings, including the royal visit by Edward VII to the system in 1902, did entail passenger trains. However, it was primarily a freight network feeding into the main line. At one time freight trains ran from Burton upon Trent to all parts of the country, including daily services to London, the

wagons and barrels being lowered into a bonded store underneath St Pancras station.

The flat area of Burton town centre resulted in about 30 level crossings. Although measures were taken to reduce delay to road traffic, such as ensuring trains were neither too long, nor too slow, congestion could and did occur. After World War 2 a gradual reduction in the number of breweries, together with a virtual abandonment of the use of rail transport, resulted in the elimination of the private brewery lines at Burton upon Trent. Steam operation had ended by 1964 and by 1967 most lines were out of use. Today the rail links that once criss-crossed the town centre and held up the traffic in Station Street and the High Street are no more, yet the traffic is still congested!

Right: The beer from Burton upon Trent was distributed throughout the country and at one time a number of trains ran daily to St Pancras. The beer store below the London station's platforms was specially designed, the 720 supports being 29ft 4in apart, to allow the maximum number of barrels to be stored between them. The store and its lines are now closed. *British Railways*

11 In Staffordshire Valleys

The North Staffordshire Railway (NSR) displayed on its heraldic crest the Staffordshire Knot and became known as the 'Knotty'. The railway served the industrial Potteries, together with some of the most beautiful rural areas in England. Its 27¾ mile line

Its 27¾ mile line through much of the Churnet Valley ran from North Rode, south of Macclesfield, to Uttoxeter via Leek. Indeed this route travelled through an area south of Cheddleton which was known as Staffordshire's 'Little Switzerland'. The line

ALTON TOWERS
AND GARDENS
(MID-WAY BETWEEN UTTOXETER AND LEEK L.M.S RAILWAY)
FREQUENT EXCURSIONS — SEE HANDBILLS FOR PARTICULARS
CELEBRATED BANDS PLAY IN THE GARDENS SATURDAYS & SUNDAYS DURING THE SEASON. FIRST CLASS UNLIMITED CATERING (LICENSED) OPEN DAILY INCLUDING SUNDAYS.
TRAVEL LMS
ALTON LMS STATION ADJOINS

Left: LMS poster for Alton Towers explaining there were frequent excursion to the delights of the area and of the convenient location of Alton station. Note the single digit telephone number '7'. *Courtesy NRM*

Below: The Italian influenced Alton station looking towards Leek and remaining in fine condition, largely unaltered since its construction, seen here on 7 September 1993. *Author*

Left A Leek to Uttoxeter train hauled by Fairburn Tank No 42081 arriving at Oakamoor in the summer of 1963.
P. G. Waterfield

Below centre: As if to reinforce the 'Little Switzerland' image of the area, this highly attractive crossing keeper's house has been retained at Oakamoor and was in first class condition when this view was taken on 7 September 1993. *M. Wade*

opened to passengers in July 1849 as the Churnet Valley Railway, but soon became part of the NSR. It was originally intended as a double track secondary main line link between Manchester and Derby. However, unfortunately it fell between the Midland line, which was more direct, and the line serving Stoke-on-Trent by a slightly longer route, but which had more local traffic.

The Churnet line was engineered by G. Bidder and involved tunnels just northwest of Oakamoor, between Cheddleton and Leekbrook Junction, and at Leek. The line followed the route, in part, of the old Trent and Mersey Canal from Froghall to Uttoxeter. It also connected to one of the country's earliest tramways, the 3ft 6in Caldon Low, which opened in 1777 and ran up to limestone quarries until 1920.

Other lines operated from Leekbrook Junction to Stoke-on-Trent and to Caldon Low, whilst a short electric railway afforded a connection to a nearby mental hospital until 1920. From Rocester a link ran to Ashbourne and on to Buxton.

The line served Alton which was an attraction as far back as the turn of this century and advertising at that time suggested Alton station as an alighting point for *'The Towers, Gardens and Castle'*. In a somewhat subservient tone NSR posters advised that the gardens and grounds of Alton Towers were open to the public kind permission of the Earl of Shrewsbury. Admission in 1898 was 6d (2½p). An interesting story also relates to Rudyard Lake station, as it is said that Kipling's Christian name was derived from the nearby lake of that name.

The service from North Rode to Leek was withdrawn in November 1960, although Leek to Uttoxeter trains ran on the southern section of line until January

1965. Freight from Leek to North Rode ceased in 1964, from Oakamoor to Uttoxeter the following year and from Leekbrook to Leek in 1970. Sand traffic from Stoke via Leekbrook Junction to Oakamoor sand sidings lasted until 1988 when the line was 'moth-balled' from Leekbrook, closure of this section was in May 1993.

Leek and a number of other stations on the line have since been demolished and some parts of the track are used as footpaths. Yet this is not the end of the line. There is much that remains such as the Florentine station at Alton. Another attractive Tudor-styled station exists at Cheddleton, which is the centre of the North Staffordshire Railway Company, who

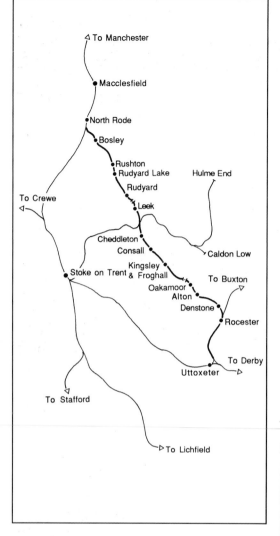

aim to run trains between Leekbrook and Froghall. A single track remains *in situ* between Leekbrook Junction and the Oakamoor sand sidings where even the diesel shunters remain in store waiting for a day when they may be returned once again to use. The track also remains extant, although currently unused, between Caldon Low, Leekbrook Junction and Stoke-on-Trent.

Although a number of engines have associations with the line, No 1, an 0-4-0 battery engine which was built by the NSR in 1917, was one of the very few battery-electric locomotives built by a main line railway. It originally replaced three horses at Thomas Bolton & Sons' copper works at Oakamoor and is now preserved at the National Railway Museum at York.

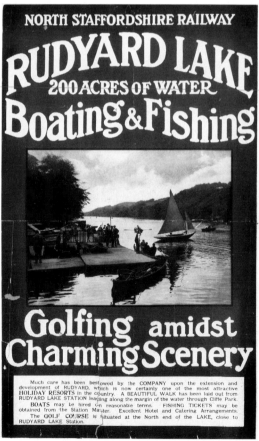

12 A Passage to Buxton

The Peak District, with its steep sided valleys and high peaks, is also sometimes known as 'Little Switzerland'. Whilst this spectacular area does not have the funicular railways of Switzerland, many lines in the area were problematical to construct, included gruelling gradients and required extensive engineering works. Buxton is the centre of the area and is an interesting spa town, which in spite of its remoteness has been used from Roman times. The town's isolation was ended by the coming of the railways, but it was not reached without difficulties for Buxton is almost 1,000ft above sea level and is the highest market town in England. Much of its later expansion was carefully planned by John Carr and Sir Joseph Paxton, under the patronage of the Dukes of Devonshire.

In addition to the physical problems, rivalry made the LNWR oppose the Midland Railway's encroachment into this area. Nevertheless, in 1860 the Midland pressed ahead with courageous plans to extend the Ambergate to Rowsley line via Bakewell to Buxton. This was a particularly difficult stretch of line through the limestone hills of the Peak District. Crossing Monsal Dale and Miller's Dale on fine viaducts and passing through 8 tunnels, the line from Rowsley to Buxton opened in June 1863. At the time Ruskin raged that 'now every fool in Buxton can be in

Left: A two-car DMU from Miller's Dale enters Buxton Midland station on 28 February 1958. The ex-LNWR viaduct on the Buxton to Ashbourne line runs left to right behind the signalbox. *J. P. Wilson*

Right: A three-car DMU from Miller's Dale enters Buxton Midland station on 5 March 1967, the last day of the service. *S. C. Dent*

Bakewell in half an hour and every fool in Bakewell at Buxton'.

A number of stations on the longer route created by this extension were also of interest. Ambergate was unique in that it originally had an arrangement of triangular platforms to serve the junction; at Matlock Bath the station was built in a Swiss chalet style; and at Rowsley the original station had been built to an appropriate style to serve the Duke of Devonshire's Chatsworth House. Finally, at Buxton the designs of the buildings for both the Midland and the LNWR stations were, to a number of elevations, identical at the insistence of Sir Joseph Paxton. The stations were located beside each other and the end walls each contained a huge semi-circular window with fan-like glazing bars.

Meanwhile a further extension from Miller's Dale

Above right: Buxton Midland station signal box on 8 March 1967. *S. C. Dent*

Right: The remains of the end wall at Buxton Midland station on 7 September 1993. Originally a fan-shaped window extended above the remaining part of the wall. *Author*

Below: The fan-shaped window still exists at Buxton's former LNWR station. The Midland's station window was once identical. *British Railways*

to New Mills and thus on to Manchester was planned by the Midland Railway and services from Buxton to Manchester via this route commenced in February 1867. However, the new link effectively put Buxton at the end of a 4-mile spur line from Miller's Dale Junction, as principal services began to develop from the Midlands directly to Manchester. Nevertheless, train services to Buxton built up and the town grew, with direct services to a surprisingly large number of destinations.

After World War 2 there was a decline in the use of the resort and most through long distance train services ceased. Through coaches ran to London, but in later years the general pattern of passenger services was for trains on the main line to connect at Miller's Dale with the Buxton branch. Miller's Dale itself was a bleak and isolated junction station almost 800ft up in the Peak, but once able to boast a post office on one of its five platforms. The spur to Buxton was the first to go and it closed to passengers in March 1967. Once the West Coast line was electrified to Manchester the line via the Peak District no longer

Above: Fowler Class 4 2-6-4T No 42366 passing Topley Pike signal box on the Miller's Dale to Buxton line with a solitary through St Pancras to Buxton coach on 25 June 1955.
T. K. Widd

Left: The tiny Blackwell Mill halt, between Miller's Dale and Buxton on 8 March 1967. *S. C. Dent*

Right: Miller's Dale Junction signal box on 8 March 1967, three days after its closure. *S. C. Dent*

Below: A landscape with trains. 0-4-4T No 41905 with the afternoon Miller's Dale to Buxton auto train crossing the River Wye on the west side of the triangular junction of the Buxton branch with the ex-Midland main line to Manchester. On the north curve, over which only limited passenger services ran between Buxton, Chinley and Manchester Central, a 4F 0-6-0 waits for the road. *A. M. Ross*

Below: 'Black 5' No 45188 passes the extensive five platforms of Miller's Dale station with an 'up' freight on 21 May 1966. *B. Stephenson*

Right: The same bridges at Miller's Dale on 7 September 1993. The 'Black Five' above had just entered the bridge to the left of this photograph. *Author*

provided an indispensable alternative route and Manchester to St Pancras trains survived only until July 1968. In February 1971 the line reopened for a temporary period in connection with the Derby Research Depot, after which the main line track south of Great Rocks Junction, which is located just north of Miller's Dale, to Matlock was removed.

One of the shocks of the Beeching Report was that

Left: A Miller's Dale to Buxton DMU leaving Miller's Dale station on 25 May 1959. *A. H. Bryant*

Below: Map of Buxton 1923. *Crown Copyright*

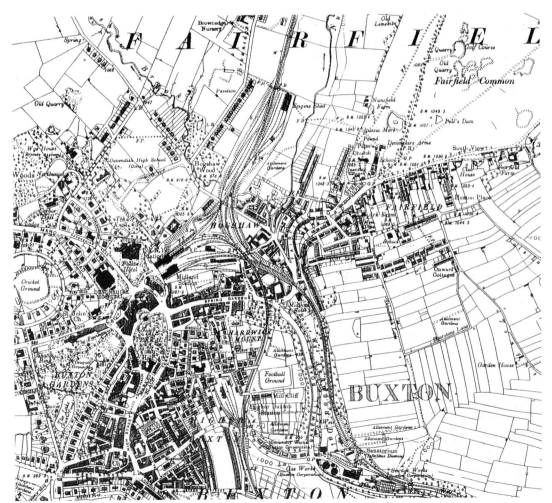

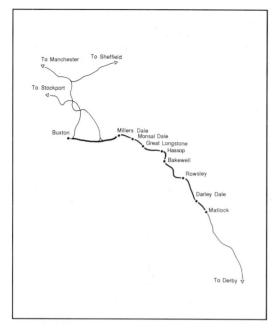

the alternative former LNWR route from Buxton to Manchester was also proposed for closure, although good sense prevailed and this route to Manchester survives. The line from Buxton to Great Rocks Junction and then northwards via Peak Forest to Chinley also remains open for freight. On the remainder of the former main line south towards Matlock sections have been turned into footpaths. Yet Peak Rail are actively restoring services from Matlock northwards into the area, with the support of the present Duke of Devonshire. The intention is to restore services right through the Peak Park, with its breathtaking views, over the 20-mile section to Buxton.

Above: Although some parts of Miller's Dale station buildings remain, much is also abandoned as this view taken on 7 September 1993 shows. *Author*

Left: The Buxton platform at Miller's Dale on 7 September 1993. *Author*

Below: 1955 timetable.

Table 213		BUXTON and MILLER'S DALE		

E Except Saturdays.   S Saturdays only.   T Through Carriages to and from London (Table 211)

Manchester was the centre of the cotton industry and was converted by the construction of the Manchester Ship Canal from an inland town to a seaport. Over the years there has been much growth and change to the stations that serve the city. There have been losses, but even where the lines have been lost a number of the main line stations have been maintained.

Liverpool Road

Manchester was linked to Liverpool by the Liverpool and Manchester Railway. This was Britain's first steam-operated main line and its station in Manchester at Liverpool Road dates from 1830. It is the earliest railway station of any size in the world to have maintained so much of its original identity. It soon became inadequate to handle the growing passenger traffic and for many years, until 1975, acted as a freight depot. It has been restored and in 1983 opened as a museum.

Central Station

The first station at Manchester Central was a temporary building opened in 1877. The permanent station was opened in July 1880 for the Cheshire Lines Committee and was used by the Midland Railway as its main terminal in the city. Manchester Central has many similarities to St Pancras; both had single span arched roofs, that at Manchester being only slightly narrower than St Pancras. There are many detailed similarities as well, including the positioning of huge clocks on the train shed end walls. Although the overall roof at Manchester Central was of classic and permanent design the offices and waiting rooms to the front were built of wood as it was proposed that an hotel should adjoin the station.

The station had a ghastly link in that Ian Brady the 'Moors murderer' met his last victim at this station in 1965. After closure in May 1969, for many years the great structure of Central station remained unused, but fortunately the classic gracefulness of its train shed was recognised and in the 1980s it was restored to become the G-Mex Exhibition Centre.

Unlike St Pancras, the Midland Hotel at Manchester Central was built across the road from the station. The Hotel was designed by Charles Trubshaw and opened in 1903. The immense brown terracotta and glazed brick exterior is increasingly regarded by many as elegant. As with a number of other railway hotels, at one time a covered way connected it directly to the station. The hotel, noted for its high standard of comfort, remains in use.

Exchange and Victoria Stations

Being frustrated by the Lancashire and Yorkshire Railway from using Victoria station, the London and North Western Railway was forced to construct its own station in close proximity at the west end of

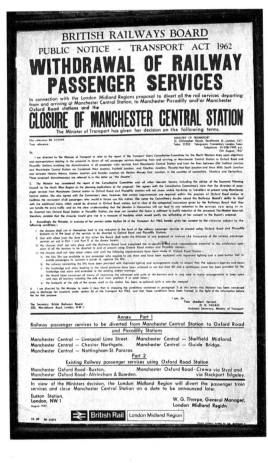

Above: Public notice referring to the withdrawal of services from Manchester Central station photographed on 2 November 1967. Closure eventually took place in 1969. *J. H. Bird*

Above: A classic view of Manchester Central on 21 December 1962. A Fairburn Tank No 42133 is seen leaving for Guide Bridge with the 2.15pm Liverpool Central to Harwich through train. On the right a 'Peak' waits to haul the 2.25pm Manchester Central to St Pancras train, the 'Palatine'. *J. Clarke*

Left: Manchester Central station presents a picture of inactivity on 5 November 1967. The two DMUs are respectively the 1.37pm to Liverpool and the 2.5pm to Warrington. The likeness of the interior to St Pancras is evident from this view. *J. H. Bird*

Victoria. The new Exchange station opened in June 1884. Exchange was primarily a terminus, with the exception of a certain number of through trains from Liverpool to stations in Yorkshire and to gain access to the LNWR lines east of Manchester. These trains exercised running powers through Victoria station. Eventually modifications were made to platform No 11 of Victoria Station were made so it extended to join up with platform No 3 in Exchange station. The total length of this platform was 2,194ft — nearly half a mile — which made it the longest platform in the world. By this alteration trains from the former Victoria platform No 11 could continue through to Exchange station, but the arrangement made for

Above: Undeterred the station and clock soon continued operation as shown in this view, dated September 1942.
Ian Allan Library

Left: After the war Exchange station was restored. This view taken on 12 March 1969 shows the rather uninspiring exterior to this particular elevation.
A. D. McBird

Above: Exchange survived the war but not the LMR. This view looking towards Salford taken on 14 February 1981, shows the station being demolished. After its closure on 5 May 1969 the station was used as a car park and the fencing posts along the edge of the former longest platform show the area so used. At the time of this photograph trains departing from Victoria's Platform No 11 still passed through the closed station using the line on the left.
Ian Allan Library

Right: An EE Type 4 No D305 awaits departure with the afternoon Glasgow train from Manchester Victoria's famously long platform No 11. *D. Birch*

quite a complicated and inconvenient walk for the uninitiated passenger.

At their zenith in the pre-World War 2 era the two stations were the busiest outside London. After World War 2 the number of trains gradually declined and as an act of rationalisation Exchange station closed in May 1969. Following use as a car park it was demolished in 1981 and the site again used for car parking. The rationalisation continues: parts of Victoria station, which suffered extensive damage during World War 2, have been considerably remodelled, and the station reduced in size by some 14 acres. Today at Victoria the number of through platforms has been reduced and the stabling of light locomotives, which used to take place on the middle tracks, has been transferred to Manchester Piccadilly.

Above: The stabling of locomotives at Victoria station on 7 August 1967. An Ivatt Class 2 2-6-0 is seen behind the more powerful 'Black 5'. *Author*

Below: The stabling of locomotives in the same spot on 27 September 1991. A Class 31 is seen behind the more powerful Class 47, a view that has disappeared with the redevelopment of this part of the station. *Author*

14 The Mersey: a tale of two stations

The River Mersey separates Liverpool from Birkenhead by a deep water estuary. With the coming of the Industrial Revolution, the development of the cotton industry and trade with America, the need for a good port became apparent and thus Liverpool developed and the surrounding area grew rapidly. Liverpool's sphere of influence increased as the railways cut through the Pennines and there was rivalry to serve both the lucrative established port trade and the urban areas that developed near by.

Liverpool Exchange

As an indication of the rivalry between railway companies, for some time Liverpool Exchange station was known as Tithebarn Street by the East Lancashire Railway and as Exchange station by the LYR, each providing separate facilities on the same site. The first station was designed by Sir John Hawkshaw and opened in March 1850. It was replaced by a new enlarged station in 1884-8 and for the avoidance of doubt as to its name, although located in Tithebarn Street, 'Exchange' was carved deep into the stone fabric.

Exchange station operated with little modification, but in a state of progressive dilapidation, for many years. It provided a landmark in British railway history when on 3 August 1968 the last steam train on a normal timetabled passenger service on BR was run into this station. In 1977 the lines running out of Exchange station were diverted on to a new underground system and a station called Moorfields was opened serving the Exchange station area. Exchange station was closed in April that year, but the listed former hotel frontage has been cleaned and incorporated into an attractive office development.

Below: 'Black 5' No 44989 waits to depart at Liverpool Exchange in June 1956. *J. Peden*

Above: Leaving Liverpool Exchange on 3 September 1976, Derby built DMUs form the 12.57 for Bolton. By this time substantial parts of the station were already out of use and much of the roof covering had been removed. *Brian Morrison*

Below: Class 502 EMU with a Southport train waiting at Liverpool Exchange, under a rather ineffective part of the roof, on 9 September 1976. *K. Lane*

Above: The front entrance of Liverpool Exchange on 9 September 1976. *K. Lane*

Above right: The frontage of Liverpool Exchange remains and has been cleaned and refurbished, including the attractive clock which still usefully protrudes from the stone-fronted building on 4 September 1993. *R. Trill*

Below: The concourse and rear of Liverpool Exchange entrance after demolition of the train sheds. The hotel remained *in situ* on 18 March 1979. *R. T. Foster*

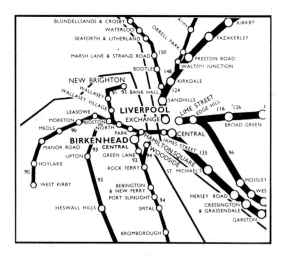

Below: 'Black 5' No 45004 at Birkenhead Woodside with the 11.45am to Paddington on 17 September 1966. *N. Matthews*

Above: A DMU waits at Birkenhead Woodside in October 1967, a month before closure. Note the interesting 'bull's-eye' windows on the main train shed retaining wall of this former GWR/LNWR joint station. *J. Clarke*

Right: On 4 September 1993 the main bridge and retaining walls at the southwestern 'throat' of the station remained, although the station itself with its impressive booking hall was demolished in 1969. *Author*

Above: A picture of inactivity at Birkenhead Woodside in October 1967.   *J. Clarke*

Birkenhead Woodside

Birkenhead, on the opposite side of the Mersey, was at the turn of the 19th century, like Liverpool, a mere hamlet. It grew as Liverpool developed, both as a suburban area and thanks to its own port and shipbuilding facilities. The original Birkenhead station at Monk's Ferry became inadequate and a new line was constructed by the LNWR and GWR through a tunnel under the town to a spacious and attractive new terminus at Birkenhead Woodside. This station was designed by R. E. Johnson and opened in March 1878.

As if to reinforce Birkenhead's reliance on Liverpool the main entrance and booking hall for the new station faced the River Mersey and the landing stage from Liverpool, yet the bulk of passengers were from Birkenhead itself and they used a rather less imposing side entrance. The station came under joint GWR and LMS administration in 1923. The GWR had its own expresses to London from Birkenhead, whilst a sleeping car ran until the service to London was discontinued as a through route. The frequent service from Liverpool to London, together with a decline in suburban services, compounded by a general weakening in the prosperity of the area led to Woodside's downfall. The station closed in November 1967. In the last days there was little traffic; the diary states:

SUNDAY 6 AUGUST 1967; Took bus to ferry, went across on a boat called the Woodchurch to Birkenhead Woodside which was a posh GW-LNWR station, but there was not a train to be seen.

The ferry boat Woodchurch is still in regular use, but the splendid Woodside station was demolished in 1969 and later replaced by offices and a bus depot. A few relics of this fine old station can still be traced, including the deserted tunnel that once led to the station. Just along the Mersey from this beautiful former railway terminus Brunel's ship the *Great Eastern* was scrapped. When it was dismantled a skeleton was found entombed within its hull which makes the fate of Woodside at one with the melancholy aspect of this part of the estuary.

15 Back up to Bacup

The Lancashire coalfield and the cotton industry (at one time the latter was the greatest in the world) began in the 1770s with inventions by Lancashire men such as James Hargreaves and Richard Arkwright. The natural environment played its part too — numerous swift streams, deposits of coal and a damp climate, for if cotton is spun in a dry atmosphere the thread snaps. These conditions resulted in the area developing as a major industrial region. It also led to the Lancashire and Yorkshire Railway (LYR) being one of the busiest of all the pre-Grouping railways. If traffic to route mileage is

Left: An ex-LYR 0-6-0 No 52440 with a Bacup to Bury train leaving Rawtenstall on 8 August 1952. Note the factory chimneys in the background for orientation with other views.
C. R. L. Coles

Below: A similar view of Rawtenstall taken on 11 February 1970. By this time the station had been reduced to an unstaffed halt. However, the train still carried mail and the sacks had to be heaved over the fence to reach the van on the right. It was said that any able-bodied passenger who helped the guard in this task was rewarded with a free ride!
J. G. Glover

Left: The site of Rawtenstall station on 14 February 1981. Note the chimney in the distance which has survived in all three photographs. The six car DMUs formed the 'Rossendale Farewell' railtour. In addition to the special headboard, the DMU also displayed a totem from Rawtenstall station. *R. G. Fox*

Below: Ex-GWR *Odney Manor* 4-6-0 No 7828 arrives at Rawtenstall on 26 September 1991 with a special train arranged for the Department of the Environment by the East Lancashire Railway. The Department has provided a number of grants towards the line. *Author*

compared to other railways, the LYR had the highest ratio.

An important constituent of the LYR was the East Lancashire Railway whose line up the Irwell Valley opened as far as Rawtenstall in September 1846. The line was extended some 7¼ miles to Bacup in October 1852, and later became part of the LYR. The topography was difficult as Bacup is about 800ft above sea level and the line was forced to reach the town on grades of up to 1 in 65. Indeed when the route was doubled in 1881 the railway had to build a second single line tunnel to the original near Waterfoot.

Nevertheless the station and yard at Bacup covered a considerable area which once included a four-road engine shed.

The area has seen industrial decline over many years and this has been reflected in the demise of its railways. Although electrification had been considered as a means of dealing with the steep gradients on the line, there was never sufficient investment available and electric trains were never introduced. Nevertheless, diesel trains were introduced to Bacup in February 1956, together with other changes and economies to both signalling and track. A frequent service used the route, but unfortunately all these measures could not save it. The line from Bacup to Rawtenstall was closed in December 1966, whilst that from Rawtenstall to Bury Bolton Street was closed to passengers in June 1972 and to all traffic in December 1980.

A second 9-mile line of the LYR, opened in 1881, led from Rochdale to Bacup. It contained the Healey Dell Viaduct which crossed the River Spod at a deep and wooded ravine. The very slender stone viaduct, which was slightly skewed, was almost 120ft high and particularly graceful. Passenger services were withdrawn on this link as long ago as June 1947 and it was closed to goods in 1967.

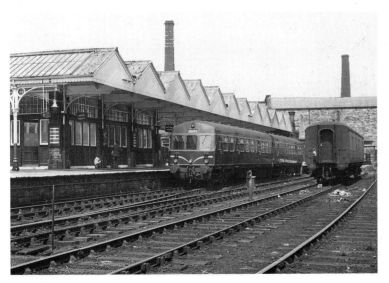

Left: General view of Bacup station with a Metro Cam DMU in the platform on 30 July 1958. *T. K. Widd*

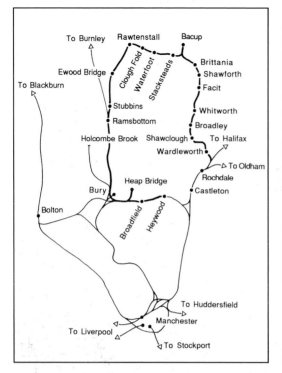

Little trace remains of Bacup station and its yard, which have been redeveloped as an industrial estate. However, the line from Rawtenstall to Bury Bolton Street and a link to existing BR lines at Heywood have been preserved by the East Lancashire Railway Society. The line provides an opportunity to see a variety of engines working this interesting route that runs to the edge of the Forest of Rossendale. This is an area undergoing 'de-industrialisation', in that lush green vegetation is returning to this once heavily damaged industrial area to recreate an attractive landscape — a landscape enjoyed by most of Lancashire prior to the Industrial Revolution.

Below: 'Farewell Bacup', one week before the station's complete closure, the Manchester Rail Travel Society tour train with Class 4 2-6-4T No 42644 waits departure at Bacup on 26 November 1966. *I. G. Holt*

Above: Despite a fifteen minute headway on Saturday passenger services by DMUs a special last steam train was run over the Bacup branch on 3 December 1966. The train, the 'Rossendale Forester' tour of the LCGB is seen here crossing the River Irwell at Clough Fold on the way to Bacup headed by Ivatt Class 2 2-6-0 No 46437 and Class 4 2-6-4T No 42644. *I. G. Holt*

Right: The line to Bacup contained interesting single bore tunnels of unequal lengths between Waterfoot and Stacksteads. The western portals are shown sealed here on 11 September 1993, but the eastern portals do not emerge together. *Author*

Above: At the other end of the East Lancashire Railway from Rawtenstall is Heywood. The 13.30pm Rochdale to Bolton train waits to depart on the last day of BR passenger services on 3 October 1970. Passenger trains returned to the station in 1994. *G. J. Jackson*

Right: A second route once ran from Bacup to Rochdale. At Healey Dell the line crossed the River Spod on an almost 120ft high viaduct. 'WD' 2-8-0 No 90568 crosses the viaduct with an afternoon freight on 15 July 1960. *R. S. Greenwood*

16 **Morecambe Bay**

The huge sweep of Morecambe Bay gives the town of Morecambe great individuality. The background to the railways and the railway hotel in the town is surprisingly complex, there being a number of stations that have closed in the town over the years. There is still one line to Morecambe, but also one line that has been lost.

During the second half of the 19th century the port of Lancaster on the River Lune kept silting up and a new coastal port was sought. The first line to reach the coast from Lancaster was in June 1848. At that time the coastal town was called Poulton-le-

Sands, but as the port developed it became known as Morecambe Harbour and by the 1850s the town was also called Morecambe. The port was in fact little more than a stone breakwater and jetty, but steamers soon began to run to the Lake District. This was followed by services to the Isle of Man and Ireland and the port was enlarged by the addition of a second jetty.

The first station was at the end of the jetty and was actually a harbour station. Although closed for general freight in 1904 and for scrap metal freight in 1933, parts remain today and the visitor can still see where

Left: Parts of the original stone pier and port station were still in existence at Morecambe on 9 September 1993 as this view shows. *Author*

Below: Morecambe Euston Road station on 13 October 1956. This view shows the considerable excursion traffic to the town at this time. The DMU on the left is from Manchester, the one in the centre is from Bury via Accrington and that to the right is from Carlisle. *A. Leather*

Above: A superannuated-looking EMU No M28222 originally from the LNWR departs from Scale Hall station on 13 October 1964. *I. S. Persall*

Below: Today passenger totals are on a reduced scale and only about 15% of visitors arrive by train. This particular departure from Morecambe Promenade, on a dull day on 9 September 1993 with a Class 142 Pacer, had few passengers. Promenade station closed in February 1994, but trains still run to Morecambe. *Author*

Right: Just part of the Gothic splendour of Morecambe Promenade station. Although part is used as a tourist information centre the listed stone station was mostly out of use when this view was taken on 9 September 1993. All tracks to this station were severed by April 1994. *Author*

Below: 'Black 5' No 44877 and BR/Sulzer Type 2 D5100 work on demolition trains at Lancaster Green Ayre sidings on 11 July 1968, just a month before the end of BR steam. *D. Cross*

Next page: Map of Morecambe 1891. *Crown Copyright*

cattle and passengers once crossed to Ireland. This first station soon became inadequate for passengers and a new station was built in Northumberland Street in 1851. This was rebuilt in the 1870s, but closed in 1907 when the Midland Railway, which in 1871 had taken over the line, opened their substantial Promenade station. It was of a typical Midland design with a Gothic air of grandeur.

A second branch to the town had been opened by the LNWR in August 1864 to a station called Morecambe, Poulton Lane. A link was also provided between the two lines, which gave the LNWR access to the existing station. However, the arrangements proved inadequate and the LNWR built a new station which opened in May 1886 when Poulton Lane closed. The new station, Euston Road, remained in daily use until September 1958 when the link line enabled trains to be concentrated at the Promenade

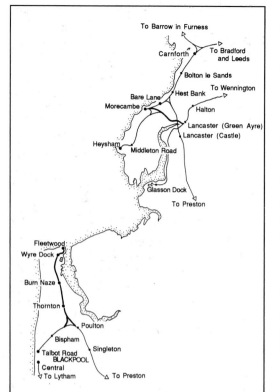

station, leaving Euston Road to be used only during the summer season. From 1960 to final closure in September 1963 its use was reduced even further to summer Saturdays only. The station was finally demolished in the early 1970s.

The Midland route from Lancaster to Morecambe and Heysham had been electrified in 1908 by use of 6,600 volts overhead contact, on a somewhat experimental basis. None the less, the original stock lasted until 1951 when it was replaced by steam. Electric traction was again used in 1953, but suspended in 1955-6. An intermediate station at Scale Hall opened in June 1957, but rationalisation meant that the passenger services on the former Midland branch between Lancaster and Morecambe were withdrawn in January 1966 in favour of the ex-LNWR route which had better connections to the West Coast main line at Lancaster. Freight was withdrawn the following year and much of the former Midland track bed is now a cycleway. In all the confusing changes the Midland Promenade station and the line to Heysham were retained by use of the link line to the ex-LNWR branch. Trains to Morecambe were replaced by buses for a period in 1994 in connection with the closure in February that year, of the listed Promenade station and the construction of yet another station in the town, some 500yd inland.

Whilst Morecambe declined as a port once

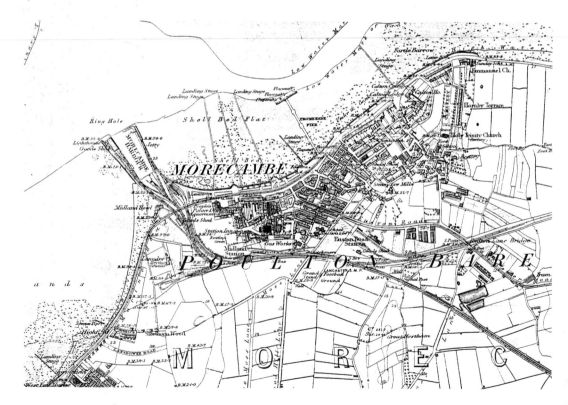

Heysham opened in 1904, it was not neglected as a holiday resort. Both the LNWR and the Midland, in particular, did much to advertise the town, which was promoted as the 'Naples of the North'. Indeed the town has a most interesting former railway hotel. The North Western Hotel was opened in 1848 and in about 1894 was renamed the Midland Hotel after the 'little' (to distinguish it from the larger LNWR outlined in Chapter 1) North Western company had been absorbed by the Midland Railway. The original building was later completely demolished and rebuilt by the LMS. In July 1933 the latter opened the present modern looking art deco Midland Hotel. This was designed by Oliver Hill with interior decor by Eric Gill. It is a listed building, remains open and is in complete contrast to the listed former station on the opposite side of the Promenade.

Right: The brand-new LMS Midland Hotel at Morecambe on 15 July 1933. *Witherington Studio*

Below: The main staircase of the Midland Hotel at Morecambe on 15 July 1933. Little has changed in the 60 or so years since the hotel opened. *Witherington Studio*

Construction of the railway line across The Fylde from Preston to the estuary of the River Wyre, which later became part of the Preston and Wyre Joint, was aided by the local MP of the name Sir Peter Hesketh-Fleetwood. His aim was to exploit the naturally sheltered inlet at the mouth of the Wyre as a seaport. He also engaged the architect Decimus Burton to lay out a fashionable resort to be named after himself.

At the time when plans for the area were being considered it was thought that locomotives would never be powerful enough to cross Shap Fell. Consequently passengers from London to Scotland would travel to Fleetwood, stay overnight at the substantial North Euston Hotel, and then travel on by boat to Ardrossan in Scotland, where a second rail trip would complete their journey. The line from Preston to Poulton-le-Fylde and on to Fleetwood opened in July 1840. A regular service of packet boats started to Scotland and also to the Lake District, the Isle of Man and Ireland, but the anticipated trade with North America did not develop.

What proved to be an important link to Blackpool from Poulton, which opened in 1846, left Fleetwood at the end of a 5-mile branch. However, in 1883 the Fleetwood line was extended from a station at Dock Street by almost 1 mile to a substantial station built right on the quayside. This provided passengers with very easy transfer to the steamers. The convenient and covered transfer made the route popular and traffic grew. Through trains ran to many destinations including London. In addition, a new spur was constructed at Poulton and opened in 1899. This allowed a frequent local train service to run directly to Blackpool from Fleetwood, Wyre Dock, Burn Naze halt and Thornton.

By 1848 the railways had overcome the obstacle of Shap Fell and any benefit of going to Scotland via Fleetwood was ended. Nevertheless, for many years Fleetwood continued to flourish as a rail-served packet port. The regular boats for the conveyance of

Below: The first Fleetwood services to Belfast were merely steam assisted sailing boats. *Ian Allan Library*

ORIGINAL TYPE, FLEETWOOD & BELFAST STEAMER, 1843.
"HER MAJESTY"
Length 160 ft., Breadth 25 ft., Depth of Hold 13 ft. 5," Registered Tonnage 312, Gross 499, Two Steeple Engines 125 H.P. each, Speed 8 Knots.

FLEETWOOD

LMS

LANCASHIRE'S GREAT FISHING PORT.

By NORMAN WILKINSON, R.I.

Right: A network of lines covered the dock area. Although this view was taken on 27 April 1951 and the Fowler Dock Tank 0-6-0T had a BR number, it still retained its LMS markings. *R. C. Casserley*

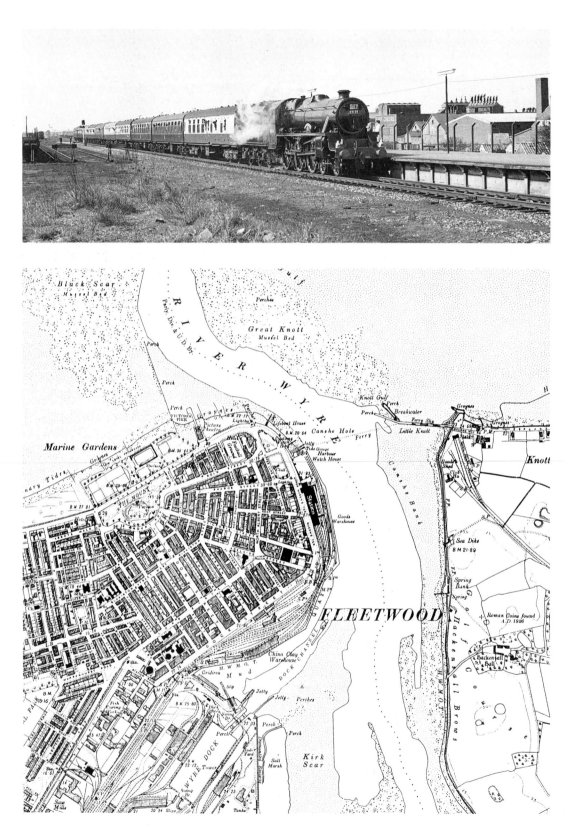

Left: 'Black 5' 4-6-0 No 45156 *Ayrshire Yeomanry* arrives at the Fleetwood branch terminus, formerly Wyre Dock, with the RCTS 'Lancastrian No 2' tour on 20 April 1968. *J. H. Bird*

Right: A tram awaits outside the North Euston Hotel on 8 September 1993. The hotel opened in 1841 and was located opposite the main Fleetwood terminus. *Author*

Below: Part of the area taken up by the old Fleetwood passenger terminus has been turned into a large public house called *The Old Station,* but by 8 September 1993 this itself had closed. *Author*

passengers and mail operated to Northern Ireland until 1928 when improvements in the service from Heysham resulted in the cessation of the Fleetwood service. Regular rail-connected services to the Isle of Man lasted until 1961 when expensive repairs to the dock could not be justified.

A fishing fleet had operated in the area since the mid-19th century, but in 1892 a trawler fishing fleet was established. By World War 1 there were over 100 steam fishing trawlers and the town developed as the largest fishing port on the west coast. Two tracks completely encircled the docks and the fish trade at one time brought substantial freight to the line, but by 1964 this had been reduced to a single train daily.

The line suffered years of decline and the vast Fleetwood terminus closed in April 1966 and for a time remained derelict, its only occupants being pigeons and seagulls. The line was cut back to a small platform at Wyre Dock, close to the original Dock Street station, but the line from Poulton to Wyre Dock closed to passengers in June 1970.

Today the vast flat expanse of the former Fleetwood passenger terminus can still be clearly traced. The docks are no longer rail-served and indeed in 1993 one of the former rail-connected warehouses was in the process of being demolished. Yet Fleetwood still has a rail connection. The Blackpool and Fleetwood Tramroad was opened in July 1898 It ran directly from Blackpool via the coast to the entrance to Fleetwood Station. It still runs today, providing at Fleetwood the only original street tramway route in this country.

18 Pennine outpost

High in the Pennines, that great and often bleak backbone of England, deep in the upper reaches of Wensleydale lies the village of Hawes, whose market and cattle fairs made it an important centre in this remote area. When the noble Settle and Carlisle line was being built across this desolate area a 5¾ mile section from Hawes Junction and Garsdale station to Hawes, which included the Mossdale Head tunnel and the listed Appersett viaduct, was carried out as one of the five contracts for the construction of the line. Hawes station opened in the summer of 1878 and Hawes became a Pennine outpost at one of the extremities of the Midland Railway. The line extended eastwards from Hawes to Redmire and Northallerton via the Wensleydale branch of the North Eastern Railway (NER). A short quarter mile section of line which connected the NER to the Midland Railway at Hawes was a joint line.

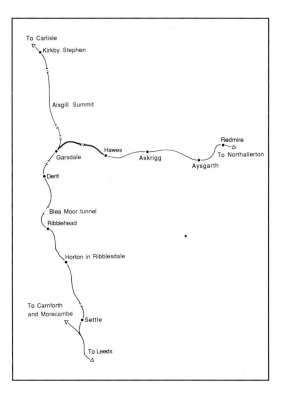

Below: Garsdale station on the Settle and Carlisle line with the former trackbed of the Hawes branch on the right, on 11 September 1993. *Author*

Right: The track diagram in Garsdale signal box on 11 February 1983. The route to Hawes branched off the main Settle and Carlisle line close to where the sidings are shown on the diagram. *G. Scott-Lowe*

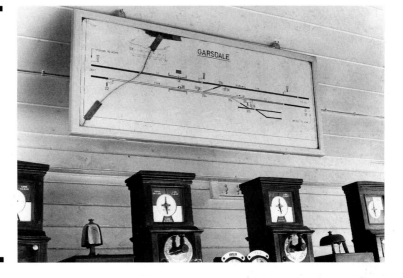

Left: Ex-Midland Railway Class 4 0-6-0 No 43960 on a Hawes to Garsdale freight on 9 March 1959. *Hugh Davies*

Right: Ex-NER Class D20 4-4-0 No 62360 piloting Ex-Midland 4-4-0 on a special train at Hawes in the 1950s. *David Laurence*

The station at Hawes was a considerable affair, built in local stone. The main passenger building was of distinctive Midland design featuring carved bargeboards and heavy glazing bars to the windows. It was a single storey building with two gables at either end facing the platform with a central gable link. A substantial stone freight shed and separate station house were also provided in typical Midland style.

Left: The derelict Hawes station in the 1970s, a decade after closure of the line through the station. *D. Pennington*

Below left: Hawes station on 11 September 1993, restored as a tourist information office and exhibition centre. *Author*

Hawes Junction and Garsdale provided the interchange station on the Settle and Carlisle line for the Hawes branch. Today this desolate and often deserted junction is a far cry from the situation at the turn of the century when the junction was a hive of activity. Trains queued to be turned on its famous turntable which had to be protected from the elements by a wall of sleepers because, almost unbelievably, a gale once spun an engine out of control, round and round, on the turntable! Such was the congestion on Christmas Eve in 1910 that no fewer than seven engines were awaiting to be turned, or were in the station area. Unfortunately two light engines on the main line were overlooked by the signalman and were hit by an express train and the ensuing fire resulted in the loss of 12 lives.

The passenger service on the Hawes line was never intensive, but in its final days the service had been reduced to just one train in each direction during weekdays. It is not surprising that such a sparse service would be unremunerative. The section east of Hawes closed to passengers in April 1954. The link from Hawes to Hawes Junction and Garsdale closed to all traffic in March 1959 and was the first section of track to be torn up, with the former junction being renamed as Garsdale. Today Garsdale remains open, whilst the buildings at Hawes, after a period of dereliction, have been converted into an information centre and exhibition. Part of the line towards Garsdale is used as a footpath.

Above: The waiting shelter opposite the main passenger buildings in the 1970s, after closure of this section of line. *D. Pennington*

Left: The same shelter after restoration and photographed here on 11 September 1993. *Author*

19 The Lakes: a line for all seasons

The combination of beautiful lakes, purity of light and dramatic variations of both colour and contour make the Lake District particularly attractive. Yet communications in the area are difficult. First, it is one of the wetter parts of the country, and in winter this precipitation can turn to snow. Second, the

Left: The 16.25 DMU from Penrith to Keswick calls at Penruddock on the last day of operation of this line 4 March 1972. *G. J. Jackson*

Below: Ivatt Class 2 2-6-0s Nos 46458 and 46426 manoeuvre on to the Keswick branch at Penrith on 2 April 1966 with the 'Lakes and Fells' railtour. *D. Cross*

arrangement of the valleys means that only one line could sensibly be run right across the area.

The Cockermouth, Keswick and Penrith Railway (CKPR) was a beautiful route operating over some 30¾ miles across the northern part of the Lake District from Penrith in the east via Troutbeck and the River Greta to Keswick. It then continued via Bassenthwaite Lake and the Derwent Valley to Cockermouth. Finally it ran some 10 miles via LNWR tracks to the coast at Workington. The route provided dramatic variations of scene in all seasons; views were particularly exhilarating from Penrith to Cockermouth and especially so if snow was around.

The line was opened in October 1864 to freight and in the following January to passengers. Traffic over the line grew and the single line section was doubled in 1900. Prior to this in 1879 Edward Tyer had tried his electric tablet system on the single line sections with such success that its use spread to many other railways. As the CKPR did not have its own rolling stock the line was worked by other railways. In particular the LNWR used the route, but on occasions the NER ran coke trains to the Cumberland steelworks. The line continued as an independent company until it became part of the LMS at the

Above: The 14.15 Penrith to Keswick DMU between Troutbeck and Threlkeld on the last day of services. *G. J. Jackson*

Below: The 15.30 Keswick to Penrith DMU approaches Troutbeck on 4 March 1972. The rear three cars formed a returning Scottish Railway Preservation Society special to Edinburgh. *G. J. Jackson*

Grouping in 1923. One of the main stations on the line was Keswick, which boasted a fine set of buildings constructed largely in local stone. Next to the station was the Keswick Hotel, built in 1869 and, as with some other railway hotels, once connected directly to the station.

Above: The 13.15 DMU from Keswick to Penrith arrives at Threlkeld on 19 February 1972 a fortnight before closure of the line. *G. J. Jackson*

Left: The attractive uncoursed local stonework of Keswick station in 1964. *J. Clarke*

Whilst the summer season services were well used and for many years there were specials and excursions with through carriages to London, the North West, North East, Carlisle and other destinations, in winter losses mounted. Some economies were made and sections of the track were singled.

Above: A DMU has arrived from Penrith on 19 February 1972 at Keswick station. Note the vast and attractive canopy over the island platforms. *D. Cross*

Right: Ivatt Class 2 No 46458 (piloting No 46426) on the 'Lakes and Fells' railtour from Manchester and seen here slowing for the tablet exchange at Braithwaite station, with Skiddaw in the background on 2 April 1966. *P. Robinson*

Left: The same Ivatt Class 2 train (as previous page) skirts the shores of Bassenthwaite Lake, between Keswick and Cockermouth, with Skiddaw rising to over 3,000ft in the background on 2 April 1966.
M. S. Burns

Below: The 9.25am Workington to Penrith and Carlisle DMU pauses at Cockermouth after overnight snow on 2 April 1966.
I. S. Carr

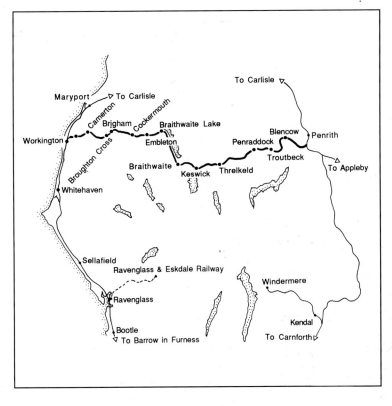

Diesel railcars took over the service in 1955; these had the advantage of providing fine views from their front and rear windows. Yet they were unable to save the line; through goods services were withdrawn in June 1964 and the line closed west of Keswick to Workington in April 1966. The remaining line closed in March 1972, although the section from Penrith to quarries south of Blencow lasted a few more months until June 1972.

A very considerable section of line between Braithwaite and Cockermouth has been converted into a road, whilst a section between Keswick and Troutbeck, together with some other shorter sections, have been converted into footpaths. A few interesting aspects of the line are preserved in the Keswick Museum.

Above: An early morning scene at Cockermouth on Saturday, 2 April 1966 after overnight snow with the 7.18am Penrith to Workington train at the platform. *I. S. Carr*

Below: The very last passenger train on the Penrith to Keswick line waits to depart Keswick with a special eight-car DMU chartered by the Penrith and Keswick Round Tables on 4 March 1972. *G. J. Jackson*

20 North Wales: coast to coast

The LMR covered much of the holiday areas of North Wales, but under the Beeching regime some interesting secondary lines, which were still relatively well used during the summer period, looked unlikely to survive much longer. The link line from Bangor on the North Wales coast, via Caernarfon to Afon Wen on the Cambrian Coast line, was one such route.

Historically the line developed as two separate parts. The first section opened was from Menai Bridge, on the North Wales main line just west of Bangor, some 7¼ miles to Caernarfon. The Bangor and Caernarfon Railway's single line ran through the Vaynol Tunnel and along the Menai Strait, via Port

Dinorwic, to a terminal on the northern side of Caernarfon. This line opened in July 1852 and soon traffic began to grow.

The second section was the 18½ mile Caernarfon to Afon Wen link. This ran from the south side of Caernarfon following the route of an older tramway as far as Penygroes, before proceeding south across the Lleyn Peninsula to the Cambrian Coast line at a point where the Afon Wen enters the sea. This section of line, which was for a time worked by the Cambrian Railway, was opened in September 1867.

Both lines were eventually absorbed by the LNWR and in 1871 they provided the logical link between the two separate sections at Caernarfon, this included a

Left: A tall ex-LNWR signalbox 'Port Siding' and a building, once part of the old Port Dinorwic station, photographed on 14 September 1961. *H. Bowtell*

Below: A special 'Land Cruise' train on a circular route from Rhyl to Corwen, Barmouth and back to Rhyl is seen here leaving Caernarfon on 26 August 1954 headed by an Ivatt Class 2 2-6-0 No 46428. The driver is noted as N. Jones. *W. G. Reas*

163yd tunnel right under Castle Square in the centre of the town. The area became increasingly popular with tourists and the following year the line north from Caernarfon to Bangor was doubled, whilst in 1894 Caernarfon station was enlarged. Caernarfon and its castle, dating from 1284, saw much activity during the investiture of the then Prince of Wales in 1911 and again of Prince Charles in 1969 and the line played a useful part in the associated travel arrangements. Furthermore, just after World War 2 the area was particularly popular with summer holidaymakers and both Brynkir and Llangybi station platforms were lengthened to accommodate 10-coach trains.

Inevitably decline set in for both freight and passengers and a number of intermediate stations were closed to passengers. The first to go was Griffith's

Above left: A Fairburn Tank No 42282 at Caernarfon with a train to Afon Wen in August 1964. *A. Muckley*

Left: Activity at Caernarfon during the summer of 1966. 'Black 5' No 45282 is on permanent way duty, taking up the Llanberis branch line. A Bangor to Caernarfon DMU waits at the platform. An abundance of cattle trucks wait in the sidings. *Ian Allan Library*

Above: Groeslon station on 26 September 1987. The old rail track on the extreme left has been turned into a cycleway. *Author*

Right: Groeslon station as seen from the train on 29 July 1964. *Author*

Left: Pen-y-Groes on 29 July 1964 with a bilingual welcoming tablet on the platform. *Author*

Below: Pen-y-Groes station looking north, ie towards Bangor in August 1964. This station was until August 1932 the junction for passengers for the 1½ mile line to Nantlle. *A. Muckley*

Crossing, on the outskirts of Caernarfon, in July 1937, followed by Dinas Junction in September 1951 and Pant Glas in January 1952. Treborth closed in March 1959 and Port Dinorwic in September 1960. The line south of Caernarfon closed, in spite of some energetic protests, in December 1964 and the track had been lifted by 1968. Between Caernarfon and Bangor the line was singled in 1966, but a comprehensive effort at both economies in operation and promotion was not really made and this section closed in January 1970.

However, 1970 was not quite the end of the story, as the line was temporarily reopened between June 1970 and February 1972 for freight as far as Caernarfon to replace the Holyhead facilities which were suspended during the closure and rebuilding of the Britannia Bridge. None the less, with the reopening of Holyhead the track was finally lifted in 1972. Even two decades after closure it is still generally recognised that Caernarfon would make a good North Wales railhead. Although Caernarfon station has been demolished and parts of the original route have been lost to other uses, there remain calls for

Above: Chwilog station, from the train on 29 July 1964. *Author*

Above right: An interesting old lamp standard at Llangybi in August 1964. *A. Muckley*

Right: A rather more overgrown Penygroes platform on 26 September 1987. Note the slight change in the present spelling of the name. *Author*

Next page: Timetable July 1955.

Table 108 BANGOR, CAERNARVON, PEN-Y-GROES and AFONWEN

Miles	Station		Week Days																		Sns.
			p.m	p.m B	a.m	a.m E	a.m Y	a.m z	a.m Sb	a.m F	a.m E	a.m P	a.m S	a.m EB	a.m S	a.m EJ	a.m SJ	a.m O	p.m K	p.m	
	99 **London** (Euston)	dep	10D45	10‡50		..	12k2	12 2	..	12† 2	m	..	B	8n15	9v20	11J15	1115	10H50	1U30	2 30	
	99 **Manchester** (Ex.)..	"	12z35	12§35		..	6k5	7 40	8 15	6E 5	8 35	..	8 35	1025	11 25	11l55	1 35	1H35	4b30	5 35	
	99 **Liverpool** (Lime St.)	"	12P10	12X10		..	7k10	7 10	..	8E25	..	9 35	..	1045	10 45	1J35	1 30	1H35	4 30	5T32	
	¶ " (Cen.L.L.)	"	..	..	..	6 15	7k35	7 35	..	8E45	9 5	..	8 55	1135	11 35	12l15	1 35	2 25	4 25	6c10	
—	Bangor	dep	4a35	5a30	9 0	9 40	1046	1046	..	11 23	1220	..	1245	2p52	3p15	4 40	4 40	5 39	7L5	9 10	Crosville Motor Buses dep Bangor (Railway Station) at 1 20, 2 30, 6 40 and 9 5 pm for Caernarvon (Castle Square)
1½	Menai Bridge		..	5 34	9 4	9 44	..	..	..	11 27	1224	..	1249	2 56	3 19	4 44	4 44	5 43	..	..	
2¼	Treborth		..	..	9 7	..	..	..	..	11 30	..	..	..	2 59	3 22	..	..	..	..	..	
4½	Port Dinorwic		..	5 40	9 12	9 50	..	..	..	11 35	..	..	1255	3 4	3 27	4 50	4 50	5 49	7L13	9 18	
8½	**Caernarvon**	arr	4 48	5 49	9 21	9 59	11 0	11 0	1123	11 44	1236	1248	1 4	3 13	3 36	4 59	4 59	5 58	7L22	9 27	
		dep	4 52	5 58	9 26	TC from Llandudno Jn. dep 9 0 am (Table 99)	TC from Llandudno Jn. dep 10 10 am (Table 99)	TC from Manchester (Exchange)	1136	11t49	1242	1255	1 7	3 17	3 42	5 3	5 3	6 2	7r28	TC from Llandudno Jn. dep 8 35 pm (Table 99)	
12¼	Llanwnda		..	..	9 37				Not after 10th Sept.	12 6	1253	Thro' Carriage to Penychain	1 20	3 28	3 53	..	..	6 13	7L39		
13¾	Groeslon		5 6	6 13	9 42					12 11	1257		1 25	3 32	3 57	5 17	5 17	6 17	7r46		
15½	Pen-y-Groes		5 13	6 21	9 50					12 18	1 6		1 31	3 40	4 5	5 24	5 24	6 24	7r53		
19¼	Pant Glas		..	6 29	9 58					12 25	1 14		1 39	3 48	4 12	..	..	6 32	8r1		
21	Brynkir		5 23	6 35	10 2					12 29	1 18		1 43	3 52	4 17	5 35	5 35	6 36	8r5		
23	Ynys		..	6 39	10 6					12 33	1 22		1 47	3 56	4 21	..	..	6 40	8r9		
24½	Llangybi		..	6 47	1011					12 37	1 27		1 52	4 1	4 26	..	..	6 44	8V15		
26	Chwilog		5 35	6 51	1016					12 41	1 31		1 56	4 5	4 30	5 46	5 46	6 48	8V19		
27½	**Afonwen**	arr	5 39	6 55	1020				1238	12t45	1 35	1 43	2 0	4 9	4 34	5 50	5 50	6 52	8V23		
32	PWLLHELI	arr	6 37	7 21	1053				..	1t7	2 4	2 4	2 20	4 30	5i5	6J18	6 18	7G20	8 45		
35½	PORTMADOC	"	6 0	8 12	1059			..	..	1 14	2 20	..	2 20	4 31	5 15	6J12	6 12	7 18	8 48		

Miles from Afonwen	Station		Week Days																			Sns.
			a.m	a.m n	a.m E	a.m Sp	a.m S	a.m E	a.m SG	a.m Sy	a.m E	a.m S	a.m xG	p.m E	p.m Z	p.m B	p.m	p.m O	p.m	p.m D	p.m	
	PORTMADOC	dep	TC Caernarvon to Llandudno arr 8 1 am (T. 99)	6 0	7 40	7 40	Not after 27th August TC to Manchester (Ex)	..	9 55	1017	1017	n	11 0	..	..	1 20	3 30	4g40	6f18	B	8 15	
	PWLLHELI	"		6 0	7 40	7 40		..	10 0	1025	1025	..	11 0	..	..	1 45	3 30	4H55	6 45	7 40	8 15	
—	Afonwen	dep		6 37	8 5	8 10		TC Caernarvon to Chester (Table 99)	1025	1045	1050	1112	1125	..	TC to Liverpool (Lime St.)	2 7	3 48	5 14	7 5	8 5	8V35	Crosville Motor Buses dep Caernarvon (Castle Square) at 12 10, 1 30, 6 0 and 7 55 pm for Bangor (Railway Station)
1¼	Chwilog			6 41	8 8	8 15			1029	1050	1055	1117	1129	..		2 11	3 53	5 18	7 9	8 9	8V39	
2¾	Llangybi			..	8 14	8 22			..	1056	11 1	..	..	..		2 17	4 3	5 24	7 15	8 16	..	
4¼	Ynys			..	8 18	8 27			..	..	11 5	1127	..	..		2 21	4 7	5 28	7 20	8 20	..	
6¼	Brynkir			6 54	8 23	8 35			1042	11 4	1110	1133	1142	..		2 26	4 13	5 36	7 25	8 25	8V52	
8	Pant Glas			..	8 27	8 40			..	..	1114	1138	..	..		2 30	4 18	5 40	7 30	8 29	..	
11¾	Pen-y-Groes			7 6	8 37	8 50			1054	1117	1124	1148	1154	..		2 40	4 27	5 52	7 41	8 39	9V4	
13¾	Groeslon			7 10	8 41	8 54			1058	1121	1128	1152	1158	..		2 44	4 31	5 57	7 45	8 43	9V8	
15	Llanwnda			7 13	8 44	8 57			..	1124	1131	1155	..	..		2 47	4 34	6 0	7 48	..	..	
18¾	**Caernarvon**	arr		7 24	8 55	9 8			1111	1135	1142	1213	1211	..		2 58	4 45	6 21	7 59	8 56	9V21	
		dep	6 50	7 27	8 58	9 12	1015	1020	1116	1140	1145	1218	1216	1243	2 0	3 5	4 50	6 25	8 5	9 1	9V25	
22¾	Port Dinorwic		6 57	7 34	9 5	9 19	1022	1027	..	1147	1152	..	..	1250	2 7	3 12	4 57	6 32	..	..	..	
25	Treborth		..	..	..	..	..	..	..	..	..	..	..	1256	..	..	5 4	..	..	..	..	
25¾	Menai Bridge		7 6	7 43	9 15	9 28	..	1035	1128	..	12 1	..	1228	1 2	2 16	3 21	5 7	6 41	8 16	..	..	
27¾	**Bangor A**	arr	7 11	7 48	9 20	9 33	1035	1040	1133	12 5	12 6	1232	1233	1 7	2 21	3 26	5 12	6 46	8 21	9 16	9V40	
103¾	¶ **Liverpool** (Cen. L.L.)	arr	10 8	1048	1258	1252	1 27	2 18	..	..	3 8	3 8	4 8	5 18	5 58	6q48	7 58	10 8	a.m	..	..	
114	99 " (Lime St.)	"	1011	12S5	..	1 5	1 59	2 38	..	3Z2	4 5	4 0	4 5	5 31	5 58	7E36	9 17	10S46	12A15	..	..	
147	99 **Manchester** (Ex.)..	"	9 56	11 3	1 14	1K37	1 50	3x16	..	..	3 24	3 35	4 31	5 38	6 10	7R37	8 47	11 1	2B23	..	..	
266½	99 **London** (Euston)...	"	..	1y20	3 5	3 36	..	..	4 55	..	6 15	6 35	6 15	8h20	9 0	9*20	..	..	3U32	..	..	

A Sta. for Beaumaris (5 miles)
A Sunday mornings only
a am
B Through Carriages between Bangor and Pwllheli
B Saturday and Sunday morns. Runs 24th July to 10th Sept.
b TC to Penychain (for Butlin's Holiday Camp) arr 12 48 pm
b Dep 3 35 pm on Saturdays
C Arr 7 12 pm on Saturdays
c 5 mins. *earlier* on Sats.
D Runs 8 mins. later on Sats. from Afonwen to Bangor
D Monday to Friday nights
E or E Except Saturdays
F Through Carriages Liverpool (Lime St.) to Pwllheli except Sats.; Bangor to Pwllheli on Saturdays
f Dep 6 43 pm on Saturdays
G "The Welshman". TC Portmadoc & Pwllheli to London
g Dep 4 57 pm on Saturdays
H Except Sats. Runs until 8th July and from 12th Sept.
h Arr. 8 35 pm on Fridays
i Arr 5 24 pm on 17th Sept.
J "The Welshman". Thro' Carrs. between London and Portmadoc and Pwllheli on Sats. (11th July to 9th Sept. only Mons. to Fris.)
J Runs 11th July to 9th Sept.
K Through Carriages Liverpool (Lime St.) to Afonwen except on Saturdays
K Arr 1 16 pm 2nd July to 10th September
k Except 17th September
L Runs 15 mins. later on Sats.
l Dep 1 35 pm 11th July to 9th September
m Through Carrs. between Llandudno Jn. and Afonwen (Table 99)
n Through Carrs. Afonwen to Manchester (Ex.)
N Dep 4 30 pm on Saturdays
n Dep 8 30 am until 30th June

O TC between Pwllheli and Bangor except Saturdays
P Sats. only. Not after 10th September
P Except Mondays and is via Crewe. Higher fare charged than by direct route
D TC Afonwen to Llandudno Jn. (to Liverpool (Lime St.) until 25th June and from 10th Sept.)
p pm
q Arr. 7 8 pm on Saturdays
R Sats. only. Arr 8 17 pm on 18th and 25th June
r 12 minutes later on Saturdays
S or S Saturdays only
T Dep 5 15 pm on Saturdays

t 6 minutes later on Saturdays
TC Through Carriages
U Dep 1 15 pm on Saturdays
V 10 minutes later on Saturdays
v Dep 8 30 am on 18th June and 17th September
X Except Saturdays. Runs 11th July to 9th Sept.
X Via Crewe. Higher fare charged than by the direct route
x Mondays and Fridays. Commences 17th June
Y Saturdays only. Runs until 25th June and from 3rd September
y TC Afonwen to Liverpool (Lime St.) (to Llandudno Jn. until 25th June and on 17th Sept.)

y Arr 1 30 pm on Saturdays
Z or Z Saturdays only. Runs 2nd July to 10th September
Z Sats. only. Runs 2nd July to 27th August
z London Road Station. Via Crewe and applies except Mondays
* Arr 9 45 pm on Saturdays
† Except Sats. Dep 11 57 pm Sunday nights
‡ Sunday nights only
§ London Road Station, via Crewe
U Arr 3 19 on Saturday morns. from 25th June (3 39 on 18th June). Arr 3 25 on Sunday morns.
¶ See Tables 113 and 99

For **COMPLETE SERVICE** between Bangor and Menai Bridge, see Table 99

Left: The site of Chwilog station on 26 September 1987. *Author*

Right: Afon Wen station, with a North Wales 'Land Cruise' train in the platform and goods activity in the background. This remote junction of the line from Bangor with that of the Cambrian Coast line has since been almost obliterated. *Ian Allan Library*

Below: Rather less activity at Afon Wen on 26 September 1987. At least the hill formations on the horizon are unchanged. *Author*

the line's reopening. This not only includes plans to reopen the section from Bangor to Caernarfon as a cycleway; there are also long standing narrow gauge aspirations to connect Caernarfon with Dinas Junction and the old Welsh Highland Railway to Porthmadog in the south. Fulfilment of these aspirations will form a coast to coast line once again.

The diary records a trip on the line:

29 JULY 1964; The state of the engine was not well. It arrived at Bangor with a side tank shooting a jet of water from a rusted hole, I offered my chewing gum as a solution and a bribe for a ride in the cab, but my offers were rejected on both counts!

Whilst it is unlikely that any future train to Caernarfon will be in such a poor state of repair, the prospect of steam once again at Caernarfon by 1996 should not be lightly dismissed.

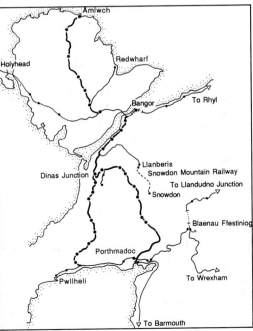

21 Anglesey against the odds

Ynys Môn, the island of Anglesey, and its railways are connected to mainland Wales over the formidable Menai Strait by the Britannia Bridge, which derives its name from a rock of that name in midstream. This spectacular bridge, built principally in wrought-iron box section by Robert Stephenson, was opened in March 1850. The entrances were flanked by two huge stone lions which are generally regarded as the finest pieces of architectural sculpture in Wales. In May 1970 disaster struck when two boys looking for birds' nests with a naked light set fire to the timber and pitch interior. The fire was of such intensity that it buckled and damaged the box sections. It looked for a time as if Anglesey might never see a train again, but a replacement bridge using the existing stone piers and retaining the lions was opened, against the odds, in January 1972.

Also perhaps against the odds, Holyhead lost its main rail freight services to Ireland, before freight

Below: The Britannia Tubular Bridge as fondly remembered. Taken on a summer's afternoon in the late 1950s 'Black 5' No 45091 heads a Holyhead to Manchester train on to the Welsh mainland. *E. N. Kneale*

Right: The first passenger train returning from Holyhead leaving the now single line bridge on 30 January 1972. The lions remain oblivious to the clutter that has surrounded them! *E. N. Kneale*

Below right: A Bangor to Amlwch auto train at Llangefni in August 1964. *A. Muckley*

Left: Llangefni station on 26 September 1987. At this time the station was in private occupation, but the line was still used for freight. *Author*

Below: An Ivatt Class 2 2-6-2T No 41226 enters Llanerchymedd station with an Amlwch to Bangor train in August 1964. *A. Muckley*

Above: Amlwch station in July 1962, a picture of activity with freight being handled by an Ivatt Class 2 2-6-2T No 41234 and the passenger train being shunted by Standard Class 2 2-6-2T No 84003. *E. N. Kneale*

BRITISH TRANSPORT COMMISSION (M)   BR 4405

LLANFAIRPWLLGWYNGYLLGOGERYCHWYRNDROBWLLLLANTYSILIOGOGOGOCH

A .70782

PLATFORM TICKET 3d.

AVAILABLE ONE HOUR ON DAY OF ISSUE ONLY
NOT VALID IN TRAINS. NOT TRANSFERABLE.

FOR CONDITIONS SEE OVER

| 1 | 2 | 3 | 4 | 5 | 6 | 7 | 8 | 9 | 10 | 11 | 12 |

ended on the branch to Amlwch. The Anglesey Central Railway opened the 17½-mile branch from Gaerwen, on the Holyhead main line, to Amlwch throughout in June 1867 and it later became part of the LNWR. The branch closed for general goods and passengers in December 1964 and Amlwch station has since been demolished. However, the line continued to be used for chemical traffic to a plant at Amlwch Port which was connected by a private line of about 1 mile in length, but this traffic ceased in March 1994. A private company has been established with the aim of returning passenger services to the branch and a number of special trains have been run.

The diary records the unusual practice of reaching the Amlwch branch from Bangor.

29 JULY 1964; The train from Bangor to Amlwch runs straight through Gaerwen, which gives you a scare that it is not for Amlwch. It then stops and reverses into the bay.

Anglesey also contains arguably the best known station in Wales, Llanfairpwllgwyngyllgogerychwyrndrobwllllantysiliogogogoch, or Llanfair PG for short! The station has had a varied career and was, in spite of its tourist potential, closed in February 1966. A temporary platform was opened after the Britannia Bridge fire in May 1970, but the station closed again in January 1972, only to reopen in May

Above: Llanfair PG. When this photograph was taken on 27 June 1971 the main platforms had been removed and the station building was used as a café. More of the platform has subsequently been reinstated and the station buildings remain. *G. S. Cocks*

1973. The station remains open, and there are plans to restore it to its Victorian glory. With some exceptions, an island that once looked as if it might have lost all its rail services has, against the odds, retained a number of them.

22 Return to Aberglaslyn

A number of secondary and usually privately owned narrow gauge freight lines were scattered throughout the LMR at its formation, but they became an increasing rarity. In Wales the Vale of Rheidol, which eventually became part of the LMR, was a notable exception. In North Wales my diary reported that in July 1964 there were several hundred small slate wagons at Blaenau Festiniog, although the Festiniog Railway had yet to return passengers to the town. However, at Port Dinorwic, at the same time,

the narrow gauge lines had all been pulled up and rails and wagons littered the former slate workings.

The 1ft 11½in gauge Welsh Highland Railway's (WHR) inclusion within the LMS had been declined and it never formed any part of the Midland Region. None the less, in terms of interest the short-lived line is noteworthy. With the backing of the local authorities in the area the former North Wales Narrow Gauge Railway, which ran from Dinas Junction to a remote spot near Rhyd-Ddu, together with the

Left: The route through the Aberglaslyn Pass was spectacular and involved a number of unlined tunnels cut through the solid rock. *Author*

Below: An incomplete Porthmadog Beddgelert & South Snowdon Railway bridge in a field near Beddgelert on 25 August 1965. *P. F. Plowman*

Porthmadoc Beddgelert and South Snowdon Railway (the latter had a number of unfinished works south of Rhyd-Ddu) were acquired. The whole ensemble was dubbed as the Welsh Highland Railway. The new company, after re–laying the track, reopened the section of line between Dinas and Rhyd-Ddu in July 1922. An 8¾ mile extension to the route of an old tramway at Croesor Junction opened the following June and the tramway was upgraded to Porthmadog. Taken together all the links afforded connection with the Festiniog Railway and formed a through line from Dinas Junction to Porthmadog.

The line ran through an area which the railway justifiably publicised for its 'Streams, Waterfalls, Lakes and Mountains'. Indeed a section ran via the spectacular Aberglaslyn Pass, located south of Beddgelert, whilst the station at Rhyd-Ddu was renamed South Snowdon for tourist purposes as it provided the shortest walking route to the summit of Snowdon. Nevertheless, the collapse of the slate industry resulted in very limited freight, the stations were located some distance from the small settlements that they aimed to serve, trains were slow and sometimes unpunctual and buses soon captured most of the passenger traffic. The winter passenger service was withdrawn in 1924 and the company went into receivership in 1927.

The line itself would have closed at the end of the 1933 summer season, but the Festiniog Railway, which still enjoyed substantial revenue from slate, agreed to lease it. From June 1934 the combined system was known as the Festiniog-Welsh Highland Railway, but it was also unsuccessful and the former WHR section closed to passengers at the end of the 1936 season and to all traffic in June 1937. The Festiniog Railway continued to run summer passenger services on its line until September 1939 and a thrice weekly goods train ran until August 1946.

Although most of the WHR track had been dismantled by the end of 1941, many of the earthworks and engineering structures associated with the line still exist. In particular several of the bridges remain, including that over the Afon Glaslyn which leads to the spectacular section carved into the side of the scenic Aberglaslyn Pass with its unlined tunnels through the solid rock and its splendid views. The aim of running trains through this section once again is being pursued. Work is already under way on a reopening plan from Caernarfon to Porthmadog. One day the railway will again return to its spectacular surroundings in the Aberglaslyn area in the

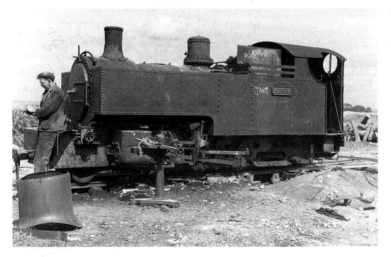

Above: The southern end of the Aberglaslyn Pass was so narrow that the railway was forced to tunnel into the side of Craig-y-llan as this view, taken 26 September 1987, shows. *Author*

Left: Russell , a Hunslet 2-6-2T dating from 1906 was unsuccessfully trimmed down to work on the Festiniog Railway's more restrictive loading gauge, becoming stuck in the Moelwyn Tunnel. On closure of the line, *Russell* spent time on mineral railways in Oxfordshire and Dorset. This view taken on 26 August 1948 shows *Russell* far away from its native line. *D. E. H. Box*

Right: At Pont Croesor the WHR replaced the original wooden tramway bridge with a steel one. Subsequently this was the only large bridge on the WHR which was removed, as this view taken on 25 August 1965 shows.
P. F. Plowman

same way that the Festiniog Railway has reopened throughout.

Although it is over half a century since trains ran on the WHR at Aberglaslyn, a number of items associated with the railway have been saved. After having been modified for work on the Festiniog Railway and later spending time at Wrexham, Hook Norton in Oxfordshire, Corfe in Dorset and at Towyn, *Russell*, one of the original locomotives on the line,

has been restored to its original condition. Today it is back on the WHR and will hopefully one day return to Aberglaslyn.

Below: After a number of years out of service, *Russell* eventually returned to traffic on the WHR in 1987 and is shown here on the short reopened section of line at Porthmadog on 13 August 1989. *T. Heavyside*

23 The lost locomotives

History happily records that Trevithick ran the first steam locomotive in 1804. The official end of the steam locomotive, on BR standard gauge at least, was a much sadder event. The last regular scheduled steam service ran on Saturday 3 August 1968 into Liverpool Exchange and the last organised farewell steam train ran on Sunday, 11 August 1968. This last train of all, which was run by the London Midland Region, attracted a great deal of attention and evoked enormous emotion.

The loss of lines in the region, compounded by the ending of steam as a general form of traction, resulted

Left: Part of the diary for 7 August 1967 states; '*Returned to Manchester and went to Central station. Steam engine at end of platform*'. Well here it is, 'Black 5' No 45150, just one of the many engines that could be seen in a single day in August 1967. *Author*

Below: The line-up for duty at Carnforth shed on Friday, 2 August 1968 — the last weekday of BR steam. 'Black 5' No 45310 and No 44781, shorn of its original number plate, sport headboards denoting the imminent demise of steam. *R. A. Cover*

Above: Bearing a wreath on its smokebox door, 'Black 5' No 45390, pilots No 45025 out of Carnforth on 4 August 1968 with an LCGB end of steam special. *B. Birch*

Below: 'Britannia' Standard Class 7 Pacific No 70013 *Oliver Cromwell* with the last special steam train run by BR on Sunday, 11 August 1968. The scene is at Ais Gill summit on the Settle and Carlisle line. The expression of the large crowd must be unique in that not a single smile is to be seen. No 70013 of the class was lucky and the engine survives. *I. S. Carr*

in a vast number of locomotives being lost for scrap. An extract from the diary shows the mass of steam locomotives, admittedly not all in use, that could still be seen on a single day trip in the North West area just a year from steam's demise:

Above: 'The End'. 'Black 5' No 45318 waits to leave Preston with the last timetabled BR steam-hauled passenger train to Liverpool Exchange. *Ian Allan Library*

MONDAY 7 AUGUST 1967: Run for train at Chester General. Railcar via Warrington to Manchester. Some steam at Helsby. Four steam trains just past Newton-le-Willows. Steam engine at Eccles and one at Salford. Steam at Manchester Exchange. Railcar to Oldham. At Miles Platting passed steam train. Near Oldham Werneth tunnel a steam engine came through. Thence to Wigan Wallgate via Bury and Bolton. Saw a Britannia class. Went to North Western station, several steam engines at this station. Also a steam engine came through Wallgate. Returned to Manchester, changed at Bolton. Steam engine at this large station. Bus to Piccadilly station, train to Hayfield. Went to Birch Vale, given some old tickets. Returned to Manchester and went to Central station. Steam engine at end of platform. No end of derelict steam trains at Northwich. Returned to Chester Northgate. Called in at Chester General and photographed a Class 9F.

All this was to change within a year. After the last steam train ran, BR for a time refused to let steam locomotives be used on its lines. Yet steam has been preserved at many locations and today the modern railway again runs steam specials. Although 1968 was the Armageddon for the 'fierce-throated beauty' on BR, there were fortunately a tolerable number of survivors and indeed the bulk of surviving steam locomotives run on a number of previously lost lines that are themselves survivors. Long may they continue.

62053

7 1 8 1 6 1 01 1 11 1 Z

British Railways Board (M)
LIVERPOOL (EXCHANGE) No. 2
PLATFORM TICKET 3d
Available one hour on day of issue only
Not valid in trains. Not transferable.
to be given up when leaving platform.
For conditions see over

1 1 2 1 3 1 4 1 5 1 6